# Windows 10 User's Guide for Beginners

**The Ultimate Guide to becoming a Windows 10 Expert in a short Time!**

# Max Anderson

disappeared. This work is sold with the understanding that the advice inside may not be suitable in every situation.

Trademarks. Where trademarks are used in this book, this infers no endorsement or any affiliation with this book. Any trademarks (including, but not limiting to, screenshots, used in this book are solely used for educational purposes.

# Table of Contents

# Introduction

Windows 10 is the latest Operating System released by Microsoft. This beginner user guide teaches you everything you need to know about this new Operating system and how it works, beginning from the type of hardware and other necessary components needed to install this Operating system into your PC, to its more advanced features. Window 10 is a combination of the best features of windows 7 and windows 8, making it even more user friendly for people on laptops, desktops, as well as mobile devices. This beginner user guide provides an in depth information on the basics of windows 10.

This user guide is written for anyone who wishes to learn about the Windows 10 OS, and especially for professionals who need to make use of this Operating system to carry out their duties in their various organizations.

Windows 10 was officially released in 2015, and was initially made available at no extra cost to those who have genuine license keys to Windows 7 and Windows 8.1. The new Windows 10 integrates the best features from the earlier windows to provide a better experience for the users on both laptop, desktop computers and those on mobile devices.

## Windows 10 Overview

Windows 10 is the realization of Microsoft's big dream to have a single windows that runs across pcs, tablets, phones, and even the company's Xbox one console. Windows 10 is mostly about fixing the mess that Microsoft created in Windows 8. One of the first signs of that is the return of the Start menu you love. It's not just the regular one from Windows 7, instead Microsoft has combined the best aspects of the last two versions of Windows to create a redesign Start menu. The live tiles from windows 8 remain, but you no longer booted into an entirely different full screen interface. There's a traditional list of apps, easy access to power options and settings, and the ability to resize the menu freely. Windows 10 has a nice dark theme and it blends in well against laptop screens that usually have black pixels. If you're not a fan of the darkness, there are plenty of color options to change the look of the Start menu and taskbar. There's even a little transparency and effects that finish off the look and feel.

Navigating around Windows 8 was painful with a laptop or PC, and Windows 10 is improved massively. The annoying hot corners of Windows 8 are gone, and Microsoft has removed the weird charms bar. In its place is a new Action Center that works as a Notification Center to collect any alerts from apps and provide quick access to a bunch of settings. Snapping apps has been a popular feature of Windows, and Microsoft has tweaked it slightly in Windows 10. There's a new snap assist feature that makes it a lot easier to find what apps are open to snap them side-by-side. There's also a new task View feature that's a lot like Mission Control on the Mac, it displays all your open windows and a single screen, and you can find what you're looking for quickly, it's also a gateway to a new virtual desktops feature. You can finally create separate virtual desktops without having to install a third-party app. it's mainly a power of user feature but it's useful if you want to separate apps on the laptop that don't have a lot of screen Space.

One of the biggest additions to Windows 10 is Microsoft's virtual assistant Cortana. It's designed to look and feel like an extension to the Start menu, just like the Windows Phone equivalent, you can use your voice to search or typing queries manually. There's even an option to enable a "hey Cortana" feature that lets you simply call the questions at your laptop. It's perfect if you lean back in an office chair and wants to fire off emails with your voice.

With a new version of Windows comes a new browser called Edge, it might have been designed to succeed Internet Explorer, but it sticks to the past in a number of ways. Edges taskbar icon is barely different from Internet Explorer in an effort to keep it similar for the millions of diverse Windows users. Edge does have some interesting new features you could draw all over webpages and send a copy to friends and Cortana appears to provide you useful information in clever little ways.

Windows 10 is a great fix to the problems of Windows 8 and it's clearly the version of Windows we'll all be using for many years as a Microsoft moves to regular updates instead of major versions every few years. It feels like the cycle of good and bad version of Windows could finally be over Microsoft might have just pulled that off Windows 10 is good and it's here to stay and that's very exciting

# Chapter 1

# What's New in Windows 10's November 2019 Update?

In November 2019, Microsoft released a new update to the Windows 10 OS, the update codenamed 19H2 is also called Windows10 version 1909. This update is the smallest and quickest so far, it is basically a service pack.To install this update to your system, go to Settings> then Update and Security> then Windows Update. You will see "check for updates". Click on it and you will get a message saying "Update Available". Next click on "download and install", and you can proceed to install the update.

According to Microsoft, the November 2019 update is a less disruptive update with fewer changes. The update contains only a scoped set of features for specific performance enhancements.

If you are tired of getting big Windows 10 updates every six months, then this November 2019 update (version 1909) is exactly what you need. Computers that have May 2019 update already installed (also called 19H1) will get a small cover through Windows update to get updated to update version 1909. So what are the features of the new Update?

## Online Search in File Explorer

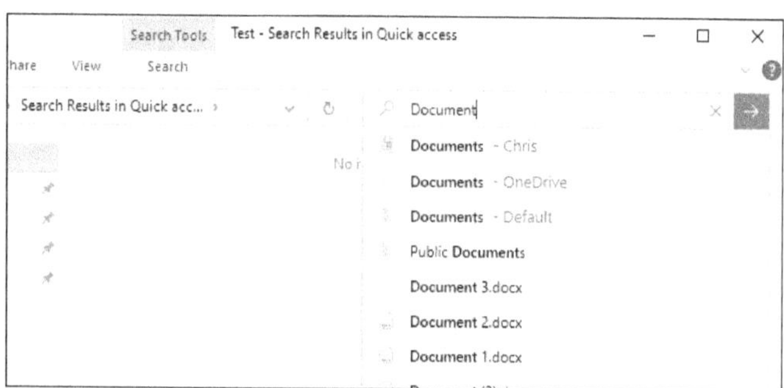

File explorer has got a sweet new search experience that is now powered by windows search. From this update, whenever you type something in the search box it will show you the drop-down suggestions it will display the result from the local files as well as from the OneDrive also. So no need to look there separately

## Other Voice Assistants now available on the Lock Screen

Before the November 2019 update, only Cortana runs in the lock screen but with this November 2019 update, you will be able to use third-party voice assistance on the lock screen these assistance will be able to hear from you and provide the answers when your PC is locked

# Calendar Event Creation from the Taskbar

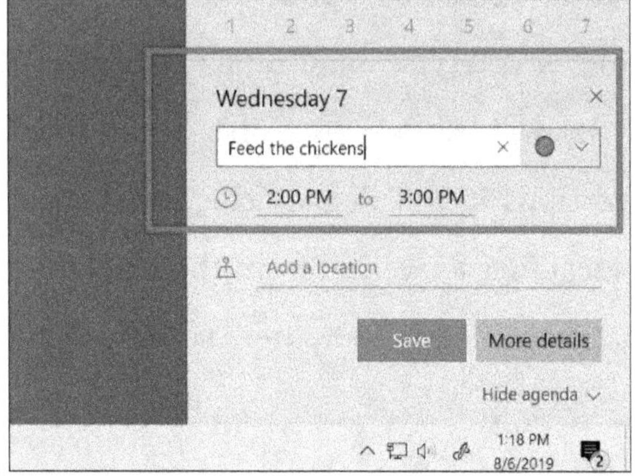



Earlier you had to open the calendar app to create an event. Now, with the November 2019 update, you'll be able to create event directly from the taskbar simply click the time and punch in your details in the panel that slides up by clicking add an event or reminder you can create a new calendar event by specifying a name time and location improved notification management

# Notification Management Improvements

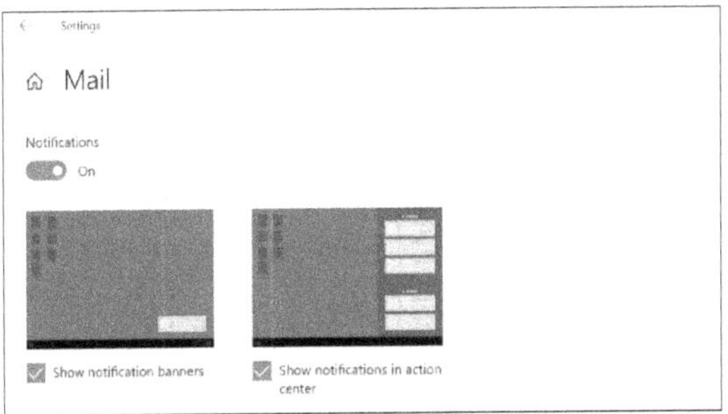

Microsoft has got a lot to do to improve the Action Center in Windows 10 though they spent some time on notifications in this update. Now, you will see the images where the notification will appear while configuring the notifications for an application you can choose to display them as banners or display them in the Action Center. In addition, the Action Center pane now has a manage notifications link that takes you straight to notification and actions pane, from there you can easily manage the notifications. You can now disable the notification sound for all apps. Before now you had to disable it separately for each applications.

## Performance Enhancements

Since this Update concentrates much on improving the quality you will see several performance enhancements in the November 2019 update. Microsoft has said that they have worked on battery life improvement, lower latency for digital inking as well as better scheduling of CPU resources. It doesn't mean that everyone will see these changes, still some PC owners will see the improvements for sure.

# Start Menu Tweaks

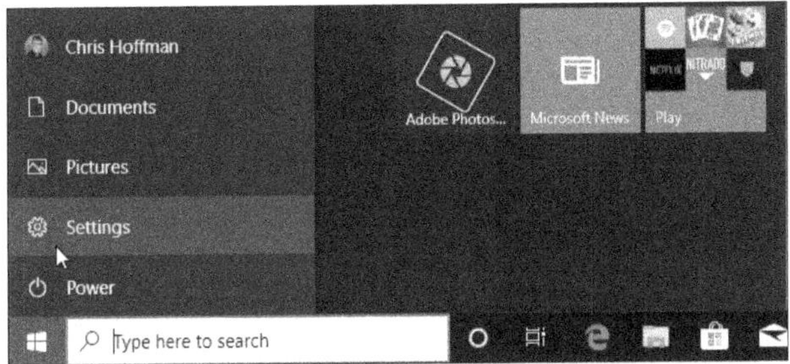

Microsoft claims it as a feature in the November 2019 update, but there are no wholesale changes in the Start menu however you will see a change that makes it more user friendly. Now, whenever you hover the mouse over the navigation area it will expand to display what you are about to click. Basically it will display what those icons are meant for, earlier it just showed the tooltip.

## Narrator Improvements

Microsoft improves its assistive technologies in every update. It is a small update, still, they have done a few things. Now, narrator and other assistive technologies can read and learn where the function key is located on keyboards, and what state it is in. this lets them determine whether it is locked or unlocked a small yet useful usability improvement.

# Installing Windows 10

Windows 10 can be installed on your computer using two major methods: Upgrade or clean install.

Generally, anytime you upgrade your OS, your files, applications and documents in your system remains unaffected, but with a clean install, all your old file will be wiped off and you need to start all over again. However, it is important that you know if your computer has the required hardware component to run Windows 10 OS effectively.

**System Requirements**

Even though most computers available in the market these days most likely have the basic requirements to run Windows 10 effectively. It will definitely be essential to know what the system requirements are just in case you need to upgrade from an older computer system.

**The major requirements include:**

- A processor having a clock rate of minimum 1gigahertz (GHz) or or faster compatible processor or System on a Chip (SoC)
- Minimum of 1-2GB of memory (RAM), however, 4GB is recommended by Microsoft
- Minimum of 32GB hard disk space

But you need to know that the installation process will authenticate your system's hardware on its own and determine if your computer meet the requirements for Windows 10 upgrade or otherwise. If it doesn't meet the requirement, then you will have to upgrade your hardware.

**Upgrading your system to windows 10 OS**

If your computer meet the requirements for a Windows 10 upgrade, you can carry out the upgrades by following these steps.

**Step 1** – Check the lower-right corner of your computer screen for a windows 10 notification. This is no longer valid and ended in 2016, it was previously offered by Microsoft to users of Windows 7 and Windows 8.1 who have genuine license keys

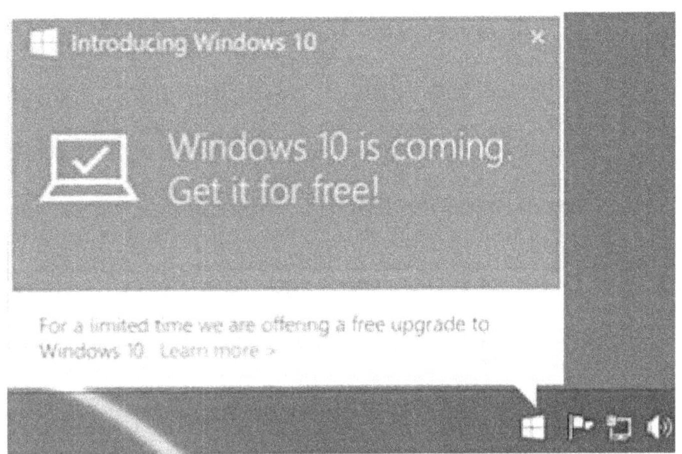


**Step 2** – once you click on the notification, the download and installation process of Windows 10 will start in your system.

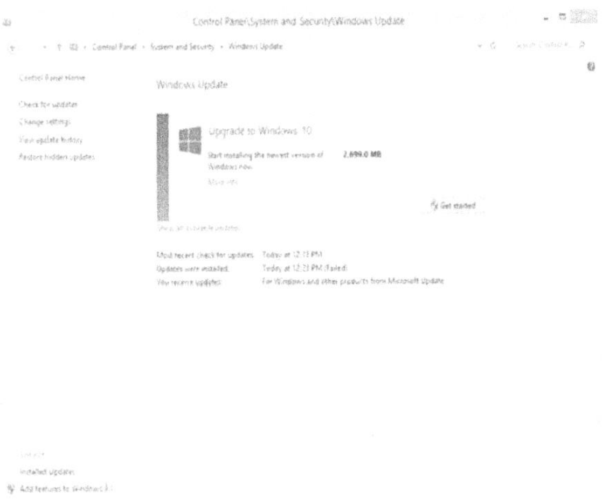

The required download file for the upgrade is a bit large, therefore, you'll have to ensure to have a good internet connection and an uninterrupted power supply for your computer to prevent interruptions during the upgrade.

**Step 3** – As soon as the download is completed, you will be asked to accept the license terms of Microsoft.

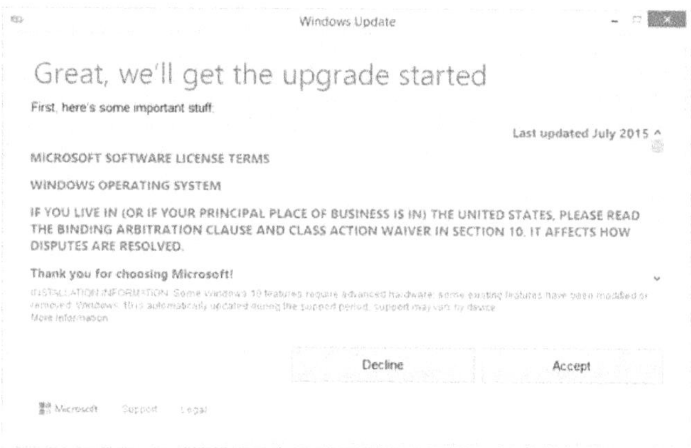

**Step 4** – Once you accept the terms, it will ask if you wish to install the upgrade immediately or do it later.

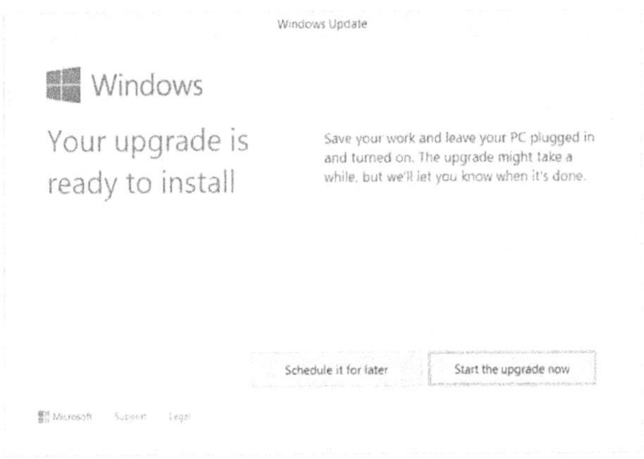


And given that the upgrade process can lasts for as long as 2 hours, it is recommended that you scheduled it for a time that is very convenient for you.

**Step 5** – Immediately the upgrade process begins, the system will carry out a number of actions, during which the following screens will be displayed.

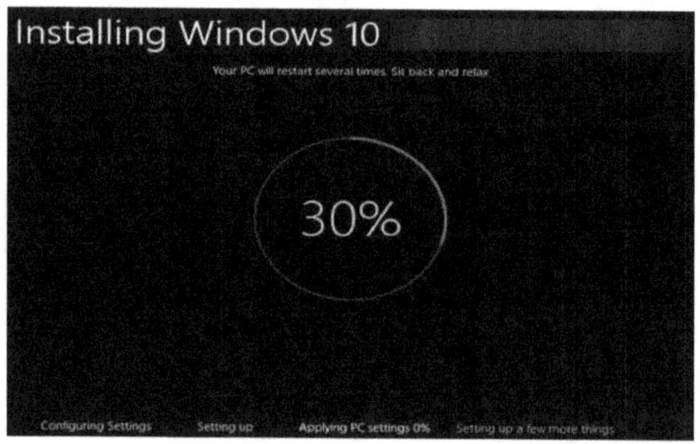


While this is going on, your computer will reboot several times, this is perfectly normal and nothing to worry about. The process is simple and it will guide you to finish the upgrade.

**Step 6** – Once the upgrade is about to finish, it will ask that you configure some basic Windows settings. You may decide to use **Express settings**, this will apply the most recommended or common settings, you can equally decide to customize the settings to suit your taste.

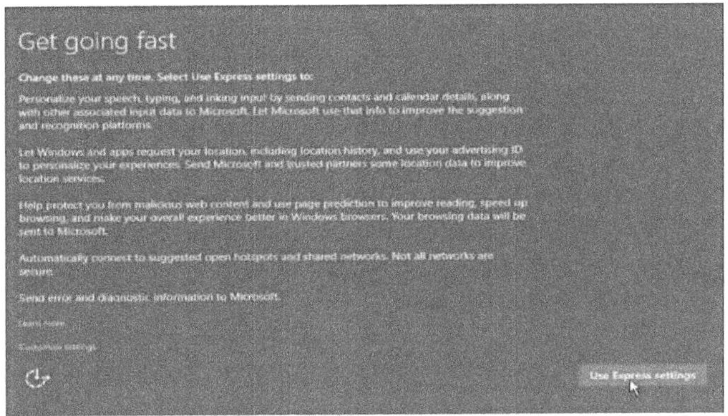


**Step 7** – as soon as the upgrade is completed, the Windows welcome screen will come up.

# Clean Install

If you are using a computer that has an older operating system such as Windows XP or Vista, you will not be eligible to do a system upgrade for free. Therefore you will have to purchase a box copy or obtain the license keys for Windows 10 for a valid installation license. The cost of Windows 10 is approximately $199.

However, note that older computers running on either Windows XP or Vista might have outdated hardware components and Windows 10 might not run on them. If such occurs, ensure that you check the system requirements outlined at the beginning of this book to know if your computer meet the requirements for Windows 10 OS upgrade.

If clean install is your preferred method of installation, all you have to do is to insert the disc into your system and powered it on. On most computers, you will need to press a particular key to boot from your CD/DVD drive, however, this can be easily achieved with F12 key on many systems. Once the disc is opened, you simply follow the outlined steps to complete the installation. They are quite similar to the steps discussed in the upgrade method.

# Chapter 2

# Getting Started with Windows 10

After you have successfully installed Windows 10, a welcome screen with time and date will be display. Simply click anywhere to proceed to the user account home screen.

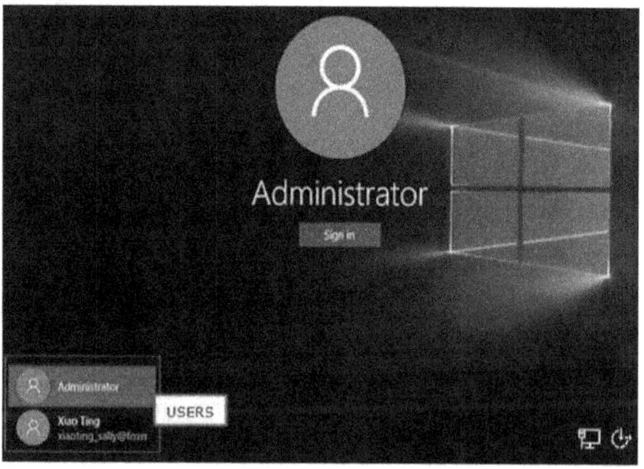



The user account scree allows you to select the user you wish to log in to, you're your screen's lower-left corner. After selecting the appropriate user, and inputting a password if needed, you will be taken to Windows 10 Desktop area.

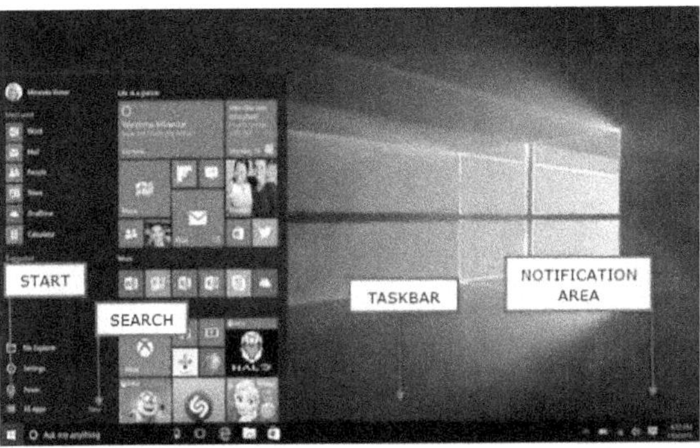


The Windows desktop is the main screen of your operating system. This is where you can locate several tools such as Start Menu, Task bar, Notification area and other Icons. There is also a search box integrated into the taskbar of Windows 10, which help you to get a great experience browsing both the web and your computer.

# Chapter 3

# Basics of Graphics User Interface

When you get to the windows desktop screen area, you will see these basic features.

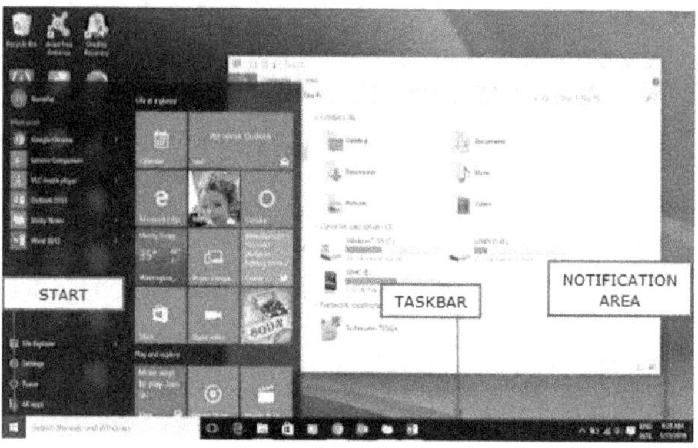



The task bar is one of the most important area of your desktop. One of the most important parts of your Desktop is the Taskbar. By default, it is located at the base of your screen, from there you can access the Start Menu, the Notification area and several application icons.

**Windows**

If an application is opened or active in Windows 10, you will notice a green line under the apps icon. Once you click the icon, the application window will be brought forward.

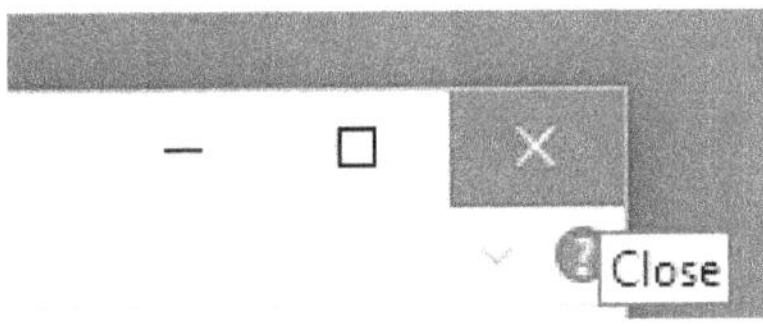


When a window is opened, there is usually three buttons display in the upper right corner of the screen, these buttons are used to maximize, minimize or close the window.

- Maximizing will make the window to have a full screen size.

- Minimizing will make the windows to hide in the task bar

You can resized or move the Windows around as you like-

- To resize any window, take your mouse to any corner till a double-sided arrow pops up, then click and drag until you get the size you desired.

- To move a window, simply click its Title Bar on click on the  Title Bar located on the upper area of the window and drag to your preferred spot

## Icons

Many Windows versions have different icons display in the Windows main screen area. An icon is basically a graphical or pictorial representation of a file or an application. To access or open any icon, simply double click the icon.

Even though the number and type of icons will be different from one computer to another, you can get more icons added to your main screen area through the underlined process:

**Step 1 –** Right-click the Desktop Background.

**Step 2 –** Select "New" and "Shortcut".

**Step 3 –** Search for the file or application or file you want to create a shortcut to.

**Step 4** – Give a name to the shortcut and click "Finish".

You can also move icons around by clicking them and dragging them to another position on your screen.

## Desktop Background

The desktop background is another major part of your desktop area. This is basically the image that is display at the back of your main screen. A lot of computers usually comes with their own background, however you can always change it to your preferred image or background.

Follow these steps to change the background-

**Step 1** – Right-click on the background and select "Personalize".

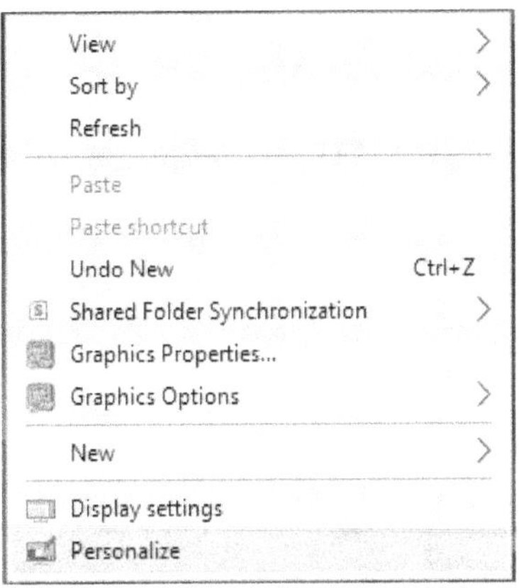

**Step 2** – when the personalization windows open, select your preferred image from the many available pre-selected images or browse your preferred one from your computer.

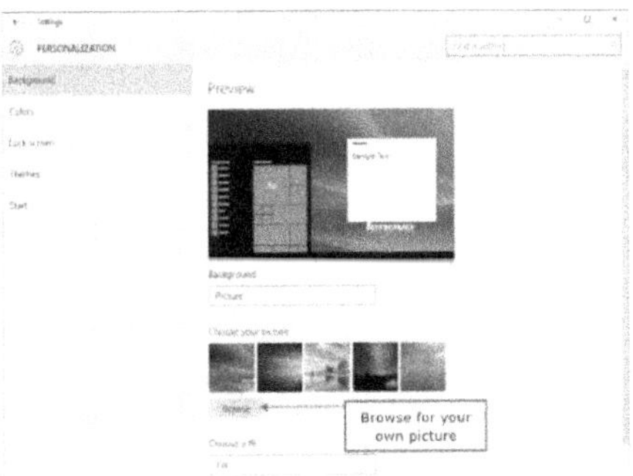


Once you select your prefer picture or image, the Background will automatically change.

# Chapter 4
# Navigating Windows 10

Navigation in Windows 10 is quite easy. All you need do is to type what you are searching for on the search area of the taskbar. It could be the name of a file, application or document, just type whatever information you are looking for in the taskbar search.

**Start Menu**

If you are searching for a particular application, you can equally open the Start Menu and click on "All Applications "This will bring out all the applications installed on your system in an alphabetical order.

## File Explorer

If you are searching for a particular document, another option is to make use of File Explorer. To do this, go to taskbar and click the folder icon.

In the File Explorer window, you can search for all your documents and folders.

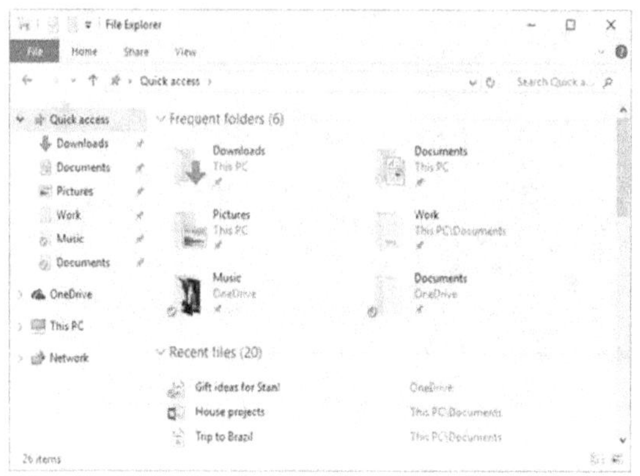

# Virtual Desktops

The addition of virtual desktops is one of the new features of windows 10. Virtual desktops allows you to have many desktop screens where your active windows can be kept arranged. You can add virtual desktop by following the steps below:

**Step 1** – go to the Taskbar and click Task View

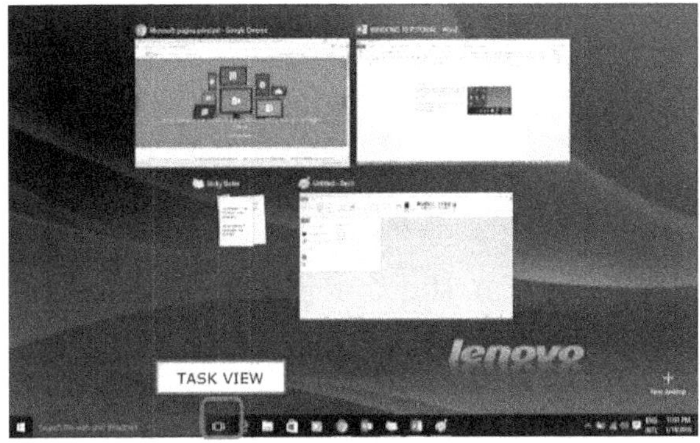


**Step 2**: on the lower-right corner, click the option "New Desktop". You can open or delete the new desktop by re-clicking task view

# Chapter 5

# The Start Menu

In Windows 10, the start Menu is the major point from which applications can be accessed. There are two primary methods of opening it.

**Step 1** – Locate the lower-left corner of the taskbar and click the windows icon.

**Step 2** – Press the Windows key on your keyboard.

There are two panes on the Windows 10 Start Menu.

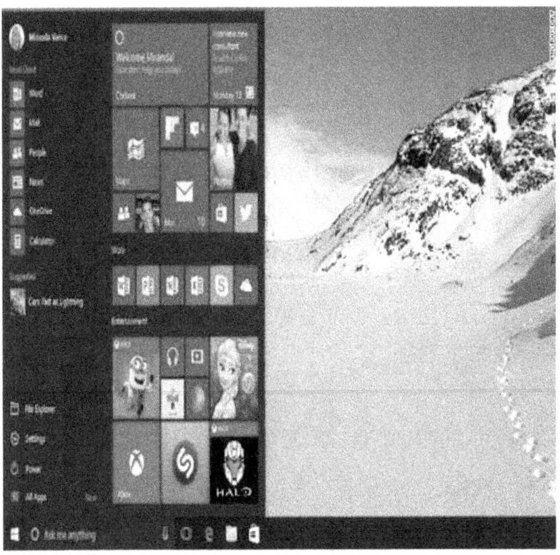

The left panes looks more like the typical Start Menu from Windows 7 and earlier windows, while the right panes have live tiles just like windows 8.

**Using the Left Pane**

You can perform a number of activities on the left pane, some of which include:

- Click your username at the top of the menu to change the settings of your account or log in with another user.

- Open the applications you use more regularly.

- A little arrow next to an application will open another menu with a list of recent documents you used that application to open.

- Open the "File Explorer" to browse your files and folders.

- Change the settings of your computer such as changing the background or Internet connection.

- See various options to shut down your computer.

- See all the applications you installed in your computer.

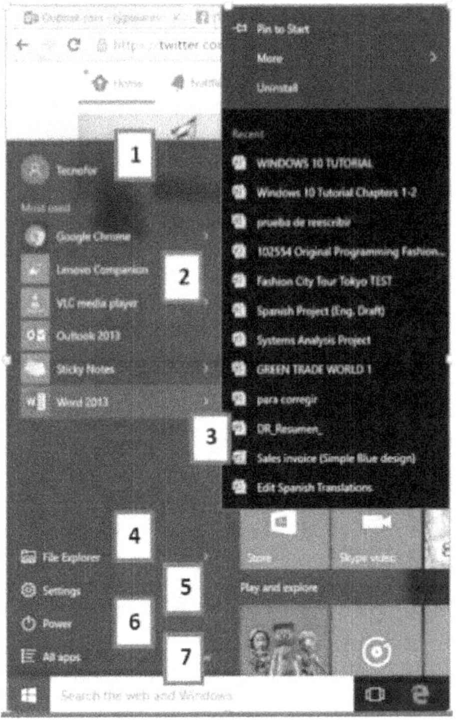

# Search Box

Using the "search box" will enable you to search within your files and documents or online for anything you have written or saved on your computer. The initial results will show up within the start menu, they will be classified according to the nearest match or matches, categorized as "Best Match".

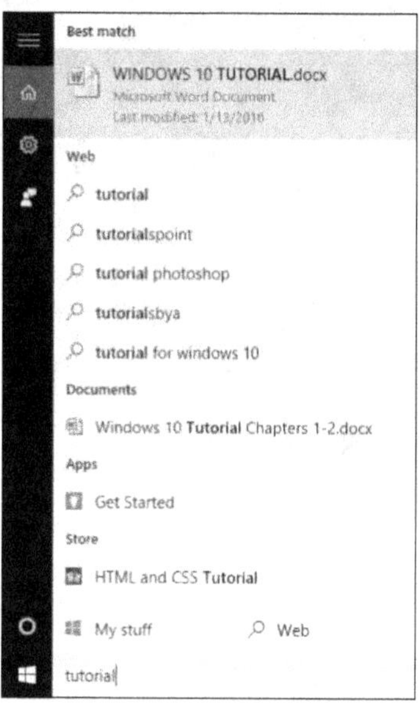

The rest of the results will be categorized according to their location or what they are

- Documents or folders
- Web results
- System Settings
- Apps

The icons located on the left side of the menu perform the following actions-

The Gear icon enables you to organize the settings of your Search.

This particular icon allows you send Feedback to Microsoft on things you love or don't like about Windows.

This is Cortana icon, it activates Windows' new personal assistant.

When you click "Web" or "My stuff" at the bottom, it gets the start menu expanded and restricts your results to the location you select, and also streamline the search.

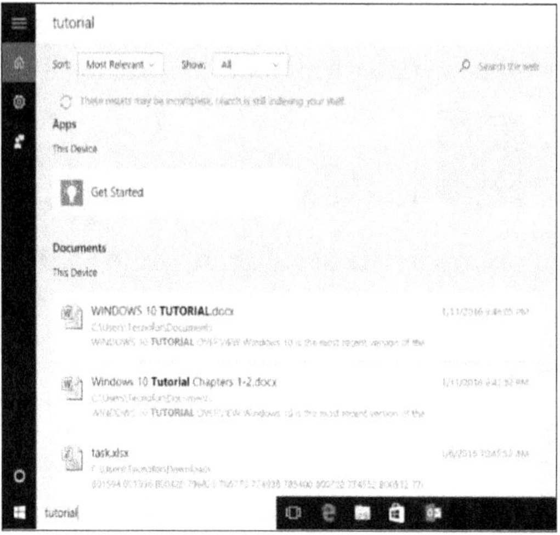

## Using the Right Pane

The right pane contains several tiles, just like the ones on the start screen of Windows 8. We can move and dragged the tiles to different positions by holding the mouse.

You can also arrange them by right clicking them to access options to unpin (remove them) from the menu or resize them.

You can also resize the whole start menu by using mouse to drag the borders to your preferred size.

# Chapter 6

# Windows 10 Taskbar

The Taskbar in Windows 10 is located at the base of the screen, allowing the user to easily access the Start Menu and Icons of the applications that are used regularly. The Notification area is located to the right of the Taskbar, it provides the user with different information such as details of the charging battery or info about the state of internet connection.

The icons located at the center of the Taskbar are "pinned" applications, this allows you to have easy access to applications you frequently use. "Pinned" applications will remain in the Taskbar till you "unpin" or remove them.

# How to Pin an Application to the Taskbar

**Step 1** – Go to the start Menu and Search for the application you want to pin

**Step 2** – Right-click the application.

**Step 3** – Choose "More" option at the top of the menu.

**Step 4** – Choose "Pin to taskbar"

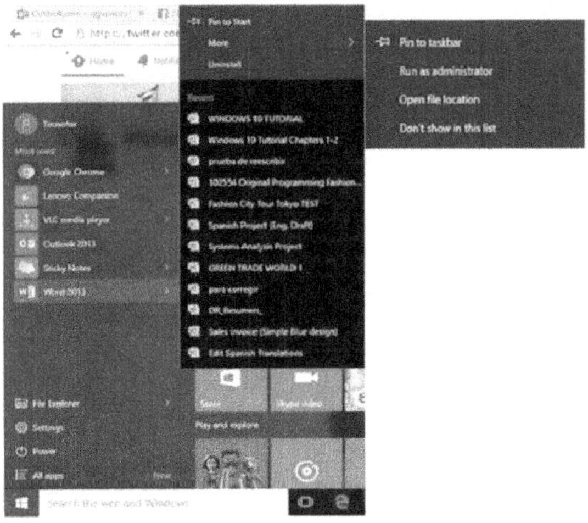

Doing this will "pin" or attach the application icon to the Taskbar of your windows 10.

## How to Unpin an Application from the Taskbar

To "unpin" an application from the taskbar, simply right-click the icon in the Taskbar and select "Unpin this program from taskbar". You can "pin" it back again whenever you so desired.

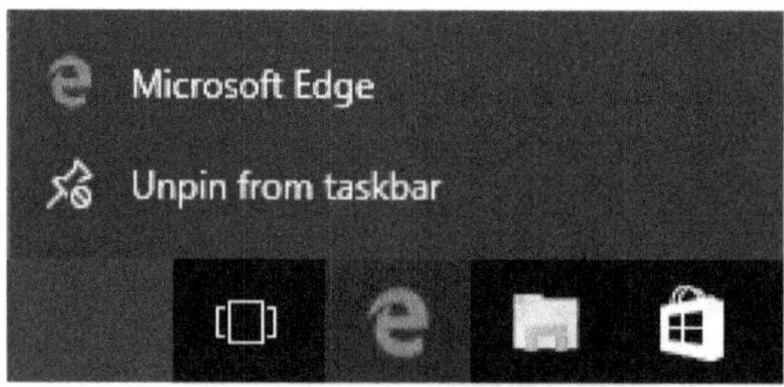


## Notification Area

Your Notification area is situated at the far right of the task bar. It displays various types of notifications coming from your computer such as volume level, battry notification or internet connection. A quick glance at the notification area will only show you few icons at first, but by clicking the upward arrow on the left side of the notification area, you will also see other icons.

## Task View

The Task View enables you to move quickly within your active applications and windows. This can be accessed via clicking the "Task View" button in the Taskbar.

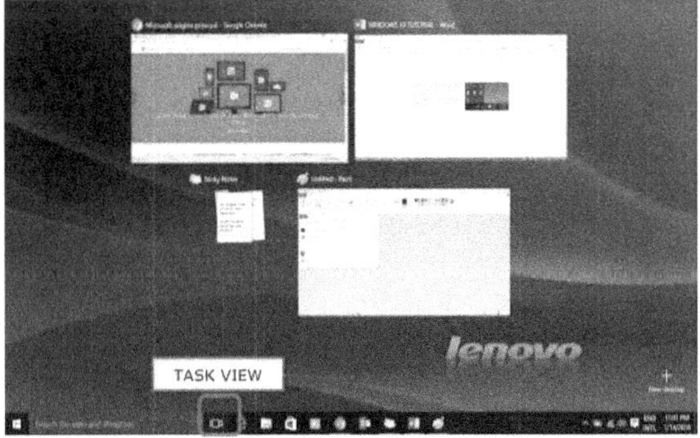


Alternatively, you can achieve the same result by pressing and holding press and the Windows key, and then pressing the Tab button

The same result can equally be achieve by pressing the Alt+Tab shortcut on the keyboard.

# Chapter 7

# Tablet Mode in Windows 10

The Tablet Mode is one of the new features introduced to Windows 10. This mode simply enables the user to change the system interface anytime a tablet is removed from the dock or base. Whenever the Tablet Mode is activated, the Start Menu becomes full-screen. While the Tablet Mode is active, other components of the windows such as the settings or the File Explorer equally open with full screen.

## How to Activate the Tablet Mode

**Step 1** – Open the Start Menu and choose "Settings".

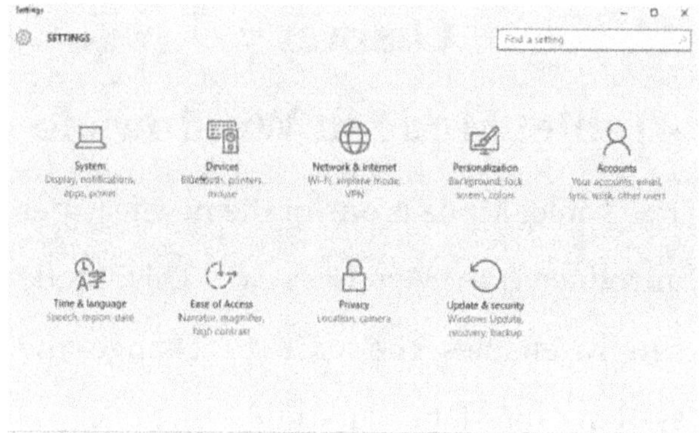

**Step 2** – choose the "System" selection.

**Step 3** – change the Tablet Mode setting from "Off" to "On".

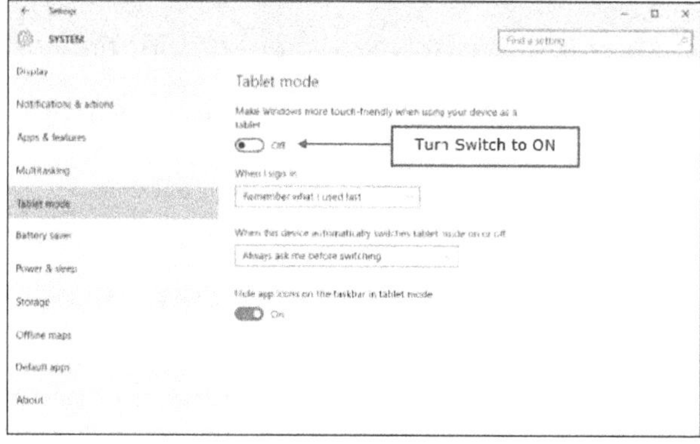

# Chapter 8

# File Explorer

The File Explorer is the application used by Windows Operating Systems to manage and browse files and folders. It provides the user with a graphical interface to access and navigate the files saved on the computer.

The primary way of accessing the File Explorer is to click on the folder icon in the Taskbar. Once the icon is clicked, the File Explorer window will open.

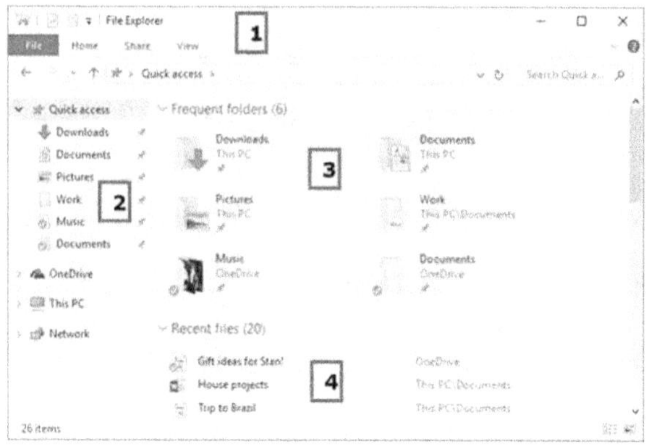

The following sections made up the File Explorer Window.

- The **File Explorer ribbon**- this looks like the ribbon in Microsoft Office. It contains buttons for tasks commonly carry out with folders and files.

- The **Navigation Pane** - This allows you to access your libraries of documents and pictures, and also your storage devices.  In addition, you can find your frequently used folders and network devices in this pane.

- The **Frequent folders**- this section is located on the right of the Explorer Window and here, you will find the folders you've recently worked with for easy access to them.

- The **Recent files**- This section is located in lower part of the windows and contains documents and files you've recently opened.

**The File Explorer Ribbon**

The File Explorer in Windows 10 contains a new toolbar, which is just like the one that comes with latest versions of Microsoft Office. The commands and buttons for the commonly performed tasks are contained in the ribbon.

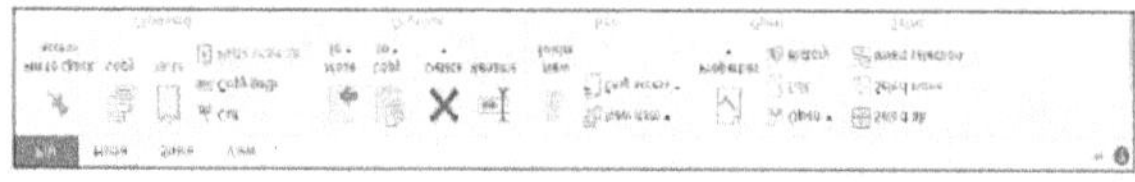

There are four tabs in the ribbon, each containing different commands. You can perform a number of tasks from the Home tab, some of which include-

- Copy and paste folders and files from one location to another.

- Open a folder or file

- Move folders and files to another location.

- Copying files and folders to a different location.

- Permanently deleting a folder or file or sending it to the Recycle Bin.

- Changing the name of a folder or file

- Creating a new folder or other new items.

- Authenticating or changing the Properties of a folder or document.

The **Share** ribbon provides you with different alternatives to share your folders and files. For example-

- Messaging or E-mailing a file.

- Compressing ("Zip") a folder to take less space.

- Faxing or Printing documents.

- Sharing with other networks or users.

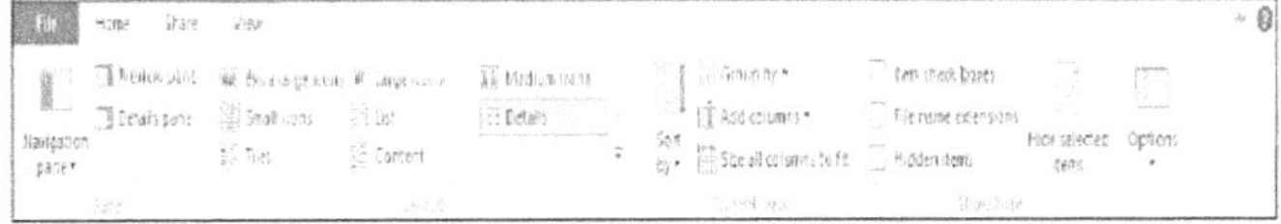

The **View** ribbon lets you change how Windows displays your folders and files. The changes you can make in view ribbon includes:

- Adding an extra panes to show details of your files or preview them.

- Hiding selected files or folders

- Categorizing and organizing the contents of your folder.

- Changing the arrangement of the folders and files from icons to tiles, list, etc.

Under the **File** tab, different menus can be accessed such as:

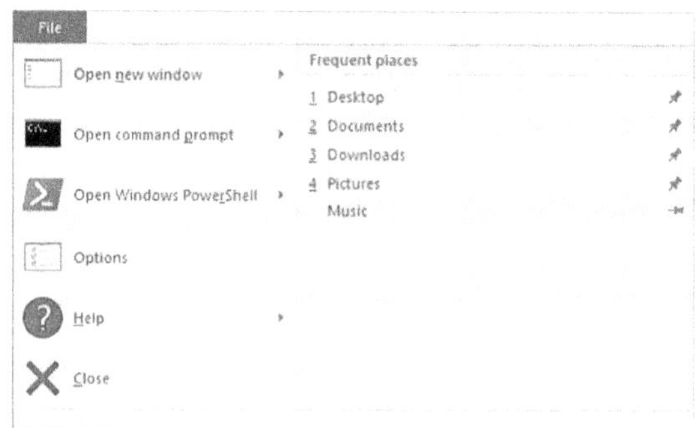

- Opening an extra File Explorer window.

- Starting a command windows for
  Pro users.

- Configuring or Changing settings
  about how File Explorer works.

# Chapter 9

## Cortana

Cortana is an intelligent personal assistant from Microsoft. It is featured in Windows 10 and other devices and systems from Microsoft such as Xbox and Windows Phones among others. Cortana will assist you to find items on your computer, scheduled appointments, get answers to your questions and lots of other things.

To use Cortana, all you need do is click the microphone icon and talk to Cortana or just type your question into the search box in the taskbar.

The icons located on the left are for:

- Home
- Notebook
- Reminders

- Feedback

**The Home** windows in Cortana is where you can ask or type questions.

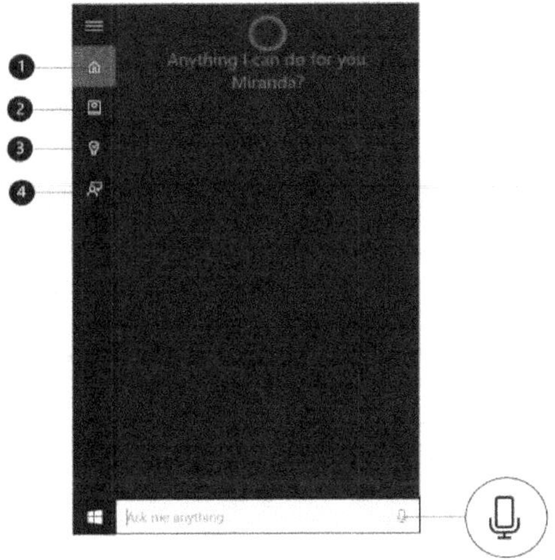


## Activating Cortana

If your Cortana is not active, you can activate it by typing "Cortana" in the search area of the Taskbar to access the Cortana settings, or simply click the "Gear" icon located on the left-side of your menu.

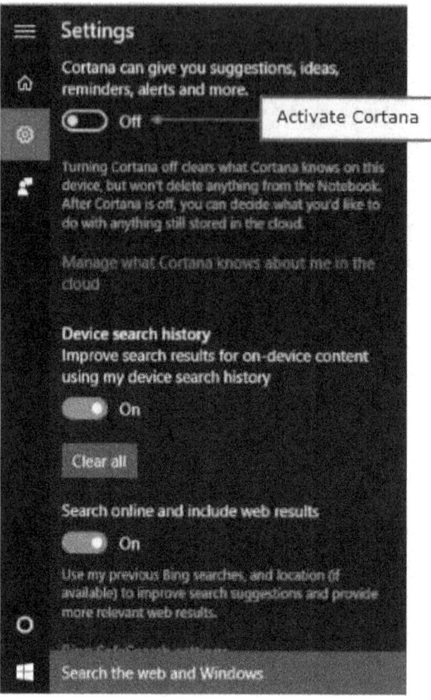


As soon as Cortana is activated, it will start collecting information about you to provide you a personalize experience.

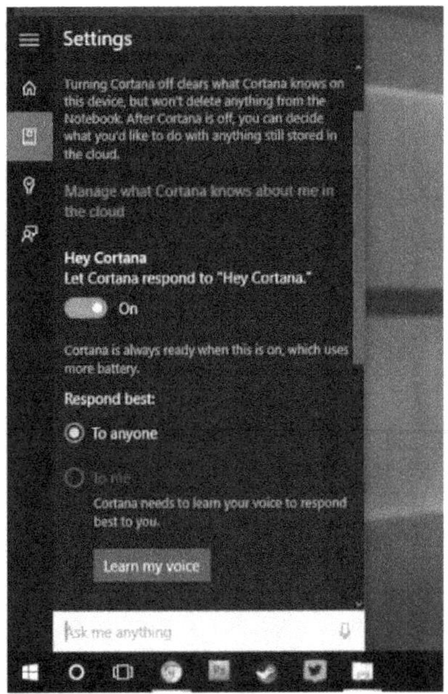

You can as well modify how Cortana interacts with you

## Personalizing your Cortana

To customize Cortana even more and enjoy even more personalize experience, you can equally open the Cortana Notebook.

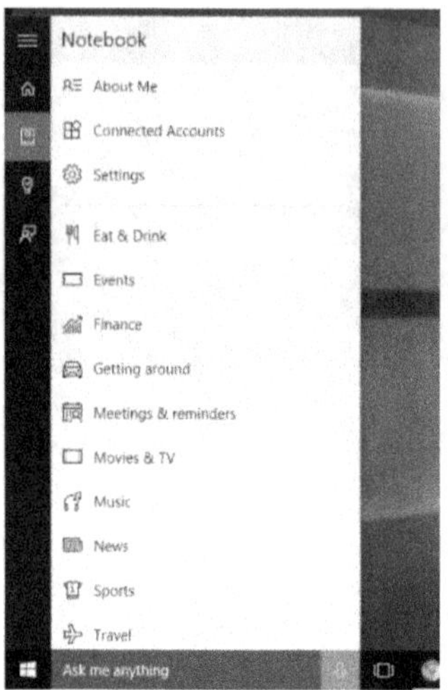

Everything that Cortana knows about you is stored in this notebook.

You can equally add reminders either by talking to Cortana or typing them.

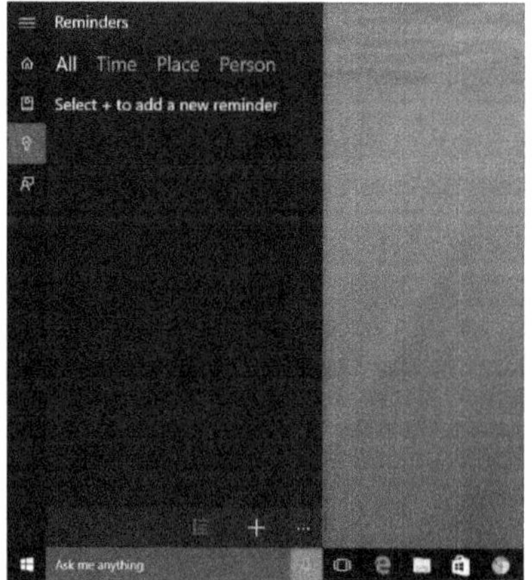

# Chapter 10

# Notifications on Windows 10

Windows 10 introduces a new way of presenting notifications. You can see this in the lower -right corner of your computer screen which serves as the notification area. .

When you click the Notification icon, a sidebar known as **ACTION CENTER** is brought forward.

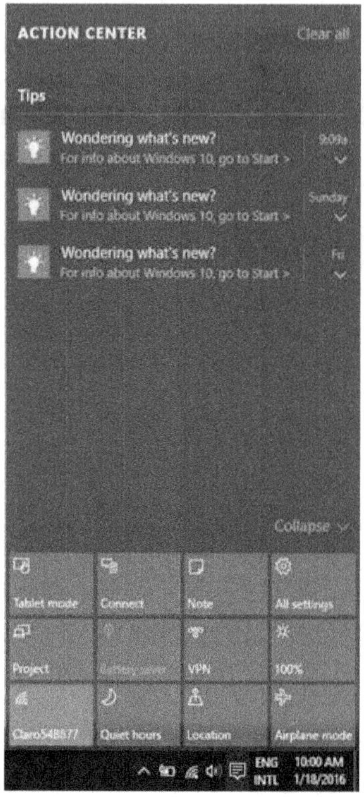


The upper area of the sidebar contains **Tips** and **App** notifications, but the lower area of the sidebar contains several **Quick Action** buttons.

# Customizing your Notifications

Windows 10 allows you to customize the type of notification you get in the sidebar. You can do this by observing the following steps-

**Step 1 –** Go to the **SETTINGS** and select **System**

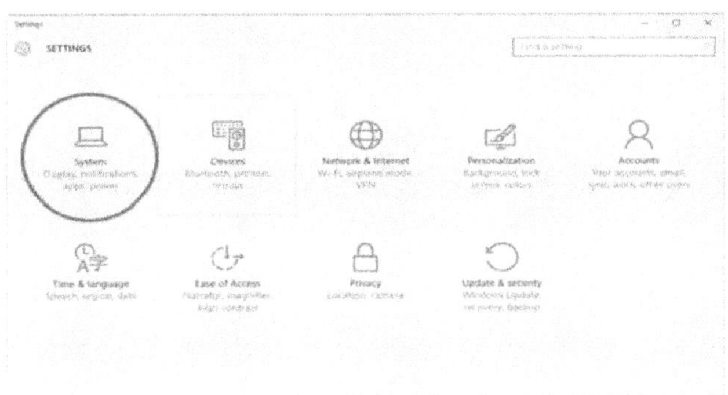

**Step 2 –** when you get to the **SYSTEM** window,

choose **Notifications & actions**. Once you do this, the screen will show you several settings where you can customize the type of notifications you want your windows to show.

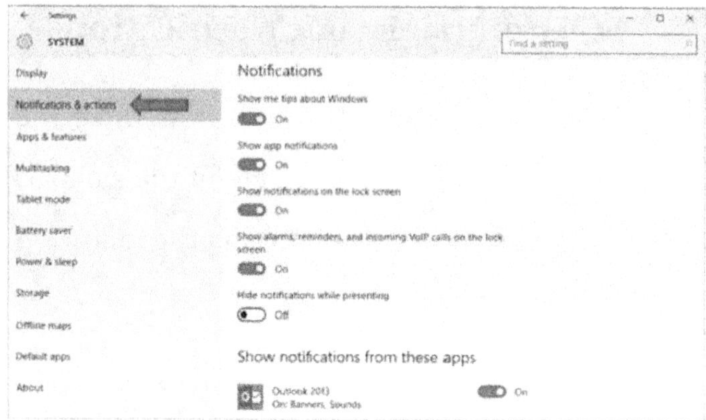

Settings
SYSTEM
Find a setting
Display
Notifications & actions
Apps & features
Multitasking
Tablet mode
Battery saver
Power & sleep
Storage
Offline maps
Default apps
About
Notifications
Show me tips about Windows
On
Show app notifications
On
Show notifications on the lock screen
On
Show alarms, reminders, and incoming VoIP calls on the lock screen
On
Hide notifications while presenting
Off
Show notifications from these apps
Outlook 2013
On: Banners, Sounds
On

# Chapter 9

# Quick Actions

In windows 10, Quick Actions are a group of tiles that allow you to easily access frequently used tasks and settings (such as screen brightness, or Wi-Fi connection).

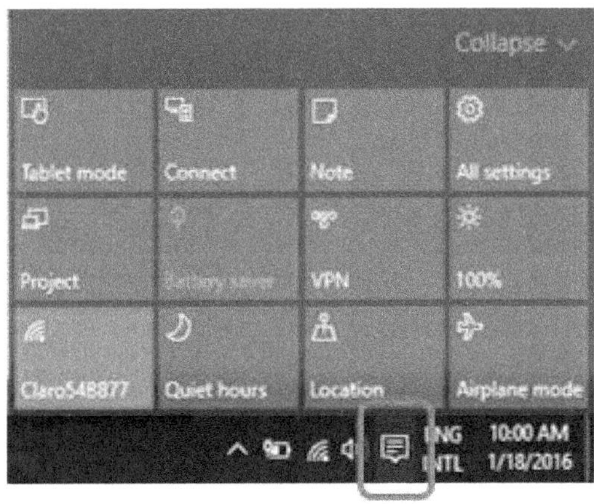

You can easily configured many of these tasks by tapping or clicking the tile. Right-clicking of the tiles will allow you to access additional options and settings.

Choosing the **All settings** tile will move you straight to the **SETTINGS** window.

## Customizing Quick Actions

The **Quick Action tiles** can be customized within notification, simply go to the **SETTINGS** window.

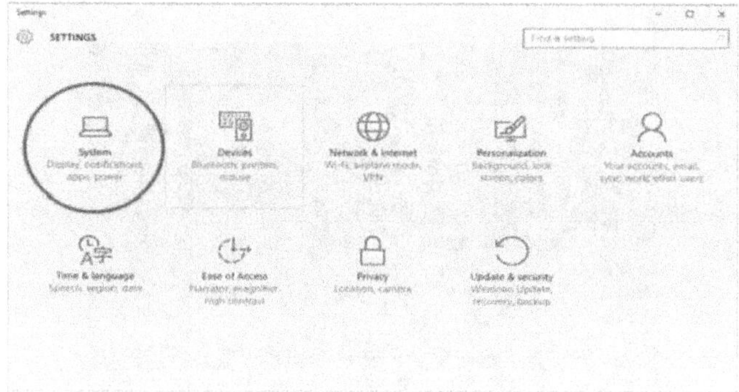

After you open **Settings**, select SYSTEM and then choose **Notifications & actions**.

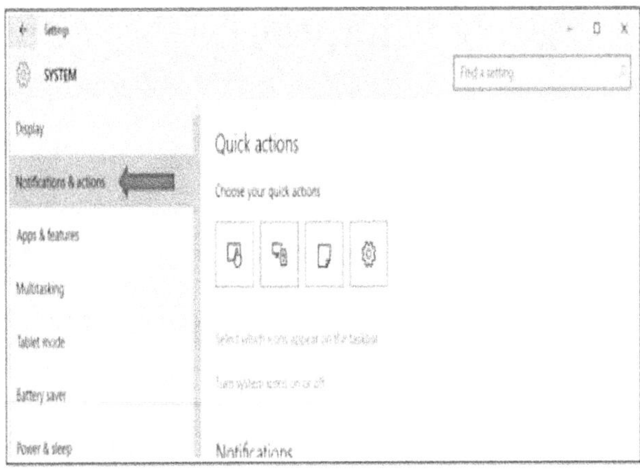


Settings
SYSTEM
Find a setting
Display
Notifications & actions
Apps & features
Multitasking
Tablet mode
Battery saver
Power & sleep
Quick actions
Choose your quick actions
Select which icons appear on the taskbar
Turn system icons on or off
Notifications

# Chapter 12

# Cloud

With windows 10, you have the opportunity to log in using an outlook account. Through this, Windows is able to synchronize your contacts, documents and other information to the cloud. The steps below will help you sign in with Outlook.

**Step 1** – Go to **SETTINGS** and select **Accounts**.

**Step 2** – In the **ACCOUNTS** window, select the option "Sign in with a Microsoft account instead".

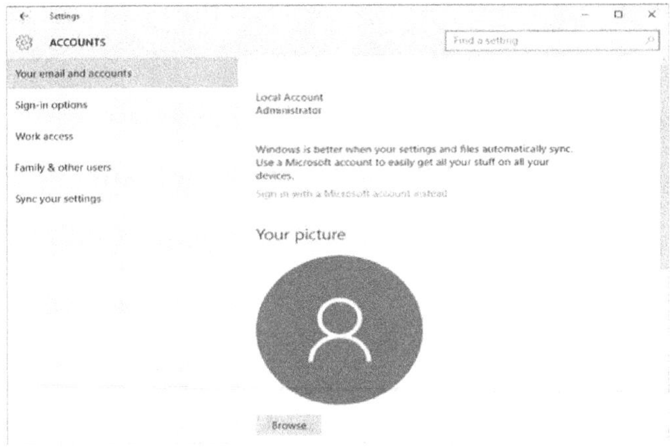



**Step 3** – The next stage is that Windows will ask you to input your username and password. And if you have no Outlook or Microsoft account, it will equally give you a link where you create your account. Using a Microsoft account will enable you to synchronize your personal files and documents to any supported device you use the account.

Make it yours

Your Microsoft account opens a world of benefits. Learn more

Email or phone

Password

Forgot my password

No account? Create one!

Microsoft privacy statement

Sign in

# Using OneDrive

When you sign in with Outlook or Microsoft account, you will be able to access OneDrive in your Windows 10. By signing in with a Microsoft or Outlook account, you have access to **OneDrive** from your Windows 10. If you have no idea what OneDrive is, it is a free Cloud storage space offered to every user of a Microsoft account.

Accessing your OneDrive from Windows is very simple, just go to the taskbar and click the Explorer Icon, this will open the File Explorer Window.

On File Explorer Window, towards the left of your screen you will see a link to One Drive

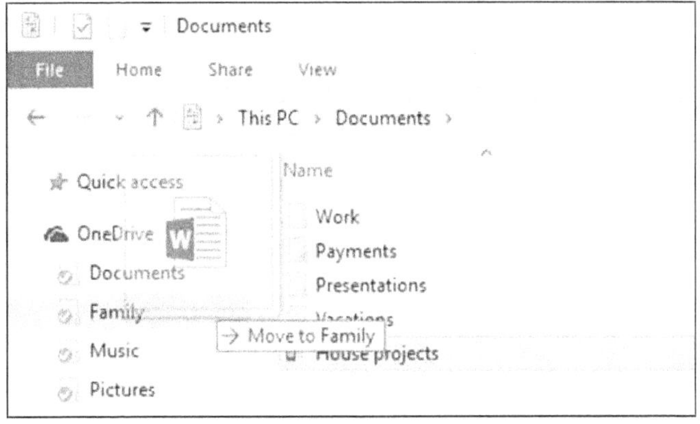

To move documents to OneDrive from your local folders, just drag them with your finger or mouse.

OneDrive uses separate types of icons to inform you about the status of your folders and files-

A blue double-arrow indicates that the folder or document is now syncing.

A red X indicate that there was some problem syncing folder or document.

A green checkmark indicates that the folder or document is in sync with the online version.

# Chapter 13

# Universal Apps

With the introduction of Windows 10, Microsoft perfected the process operating universal applications across its different platforms. What this means is that an application specifically designed for computer can as well work in an Xbox, a Windows Phone and any other Windows-compatible devices.

In order to accomplish this, Microsoft established the **Universal Windows Platform** (UWP) and improved the **Windows Store** to function as the central marketplace for all Windows applications. To access the Windows Store, simply click the store icon in the

Taskbar, the Windows Store will open and then you can browse for any application you need.

Windows equally permits "cross-buys", what this means is that when you purchase the license for an application on one device, the same license is valid on any other compatible device you have.

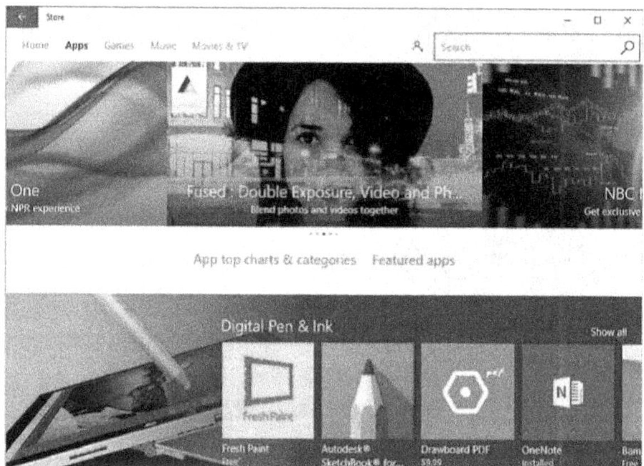

# Chapter 14

# Users Management

Like every other Windows Version introduced after Windows XP, with Windows 10, you can sign in to different user accounts on your computer. Like we stated earlier, you can select the particular account you want to sign in to after powering on your computer.

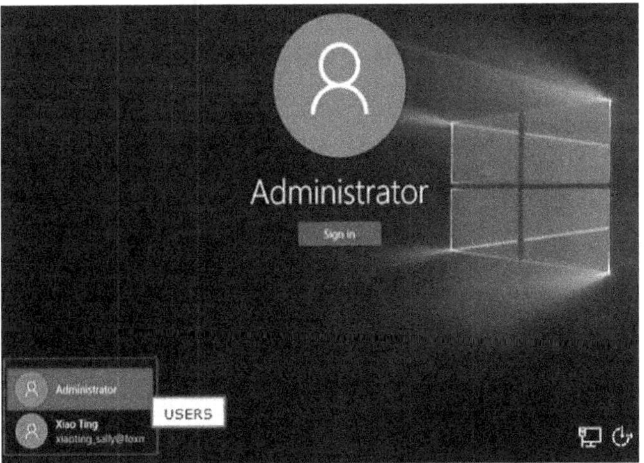


In addition, you can equally manage or configure your user account once you are logged in. in order to do this, observe the following steps-

**Step 1** – Open the Start Menu.

**Step 2** – Click on **Settings**.

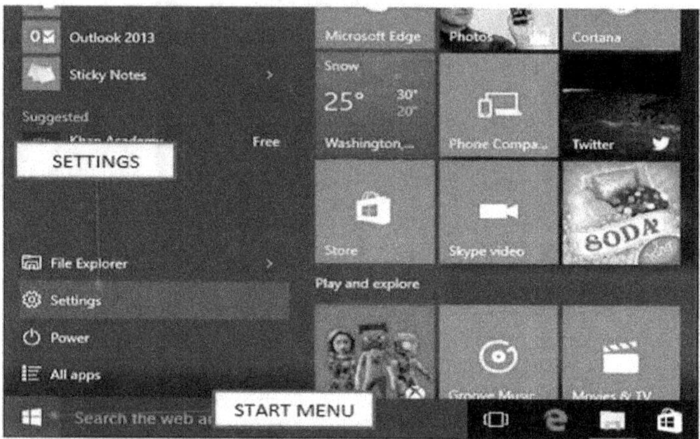


**Step 3** – In the SETTINGS window, select **Accounts** option.

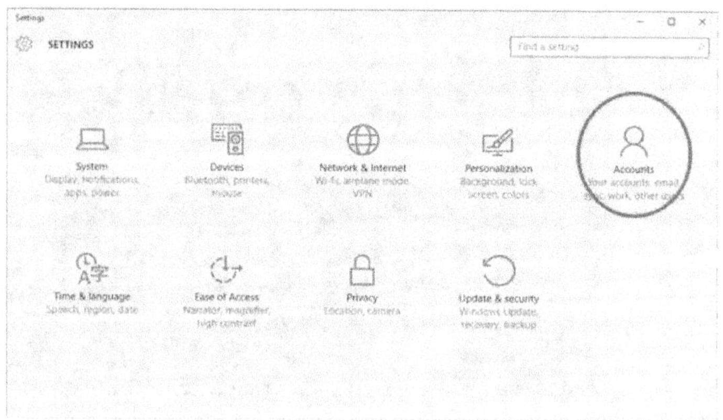


**Step 4** – next In the **ACCOUNTS** window, select the account setting you wish to configure.

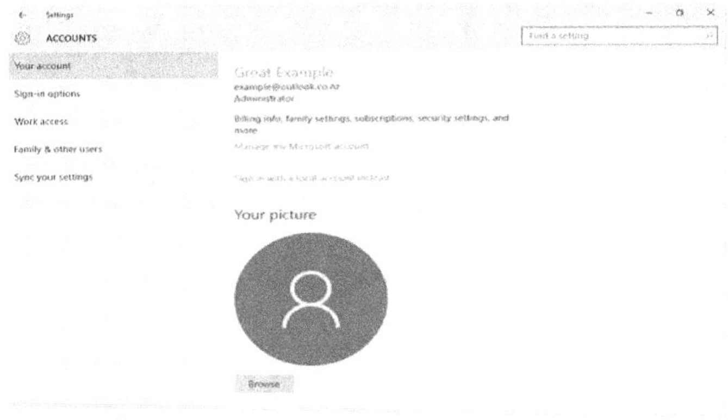

And if you wish to change your sign-in options, such as your password, choose **Sign-in options**.

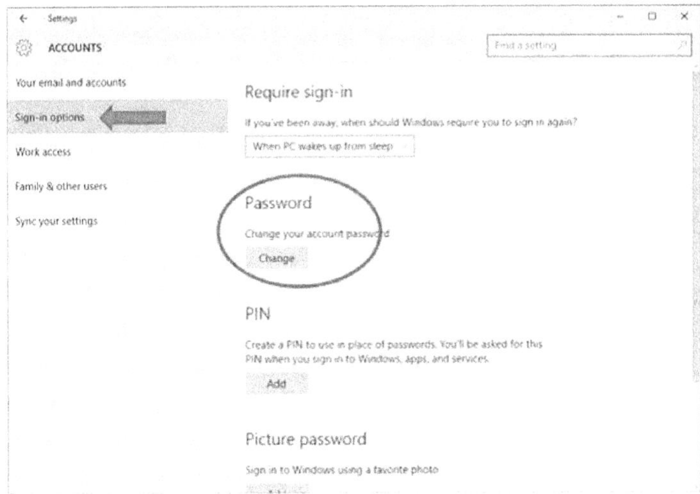

In the **Sign-in options**, Windows 10 allows you to change your password.

Likewise, it allows you select when the computer will request you to sign in.

# Chapter 15
# Security

In Windows 10, there are several tools provided to help you safeguard and shield your computer from threats such as viruses and other malwares. The three major security tools in Windows 10 include:

- User Account Control
- Windows Defender
- Windows Firewall

## User Account Control

The user account control is a Windows tool that gives you warnings when somebody or something tries to change the settings of your computer system. Whenever this occurs, you will see a warning notification on your screen until an ADMINISTRATOR confirm or approve the change. This ensures your computer is protected against inadvertent changes or a harmful software changing your settings

The User Account Control is by default set at a moderate to high level, this means that it will send you a notification only when an application attempts to make changes to the settings of your computer. But you can change this setting to the level you want by following the steps below-

**Step 1** – Open the **Control Panel**, you can easily get this by typing it into the search bar

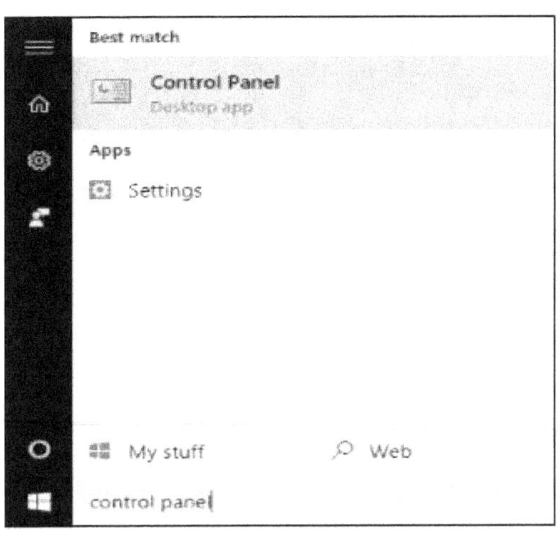

## Step 2 – Select **User Accounts Accounts**.

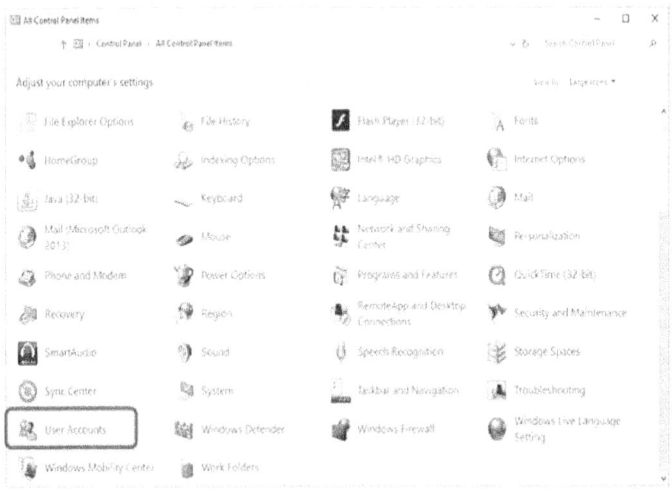

Next, select "Change User Account Control settings".

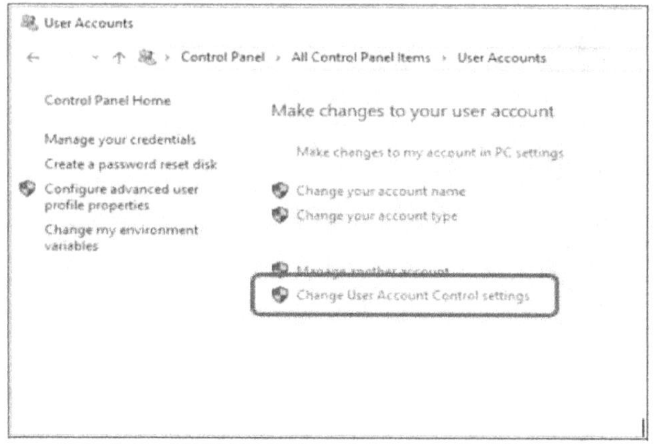

When the **User Account Control Settings**, is opened, you can drag the slider to your preferred position. Windows 10 will provide you a summary of how your computer will perform under that level.

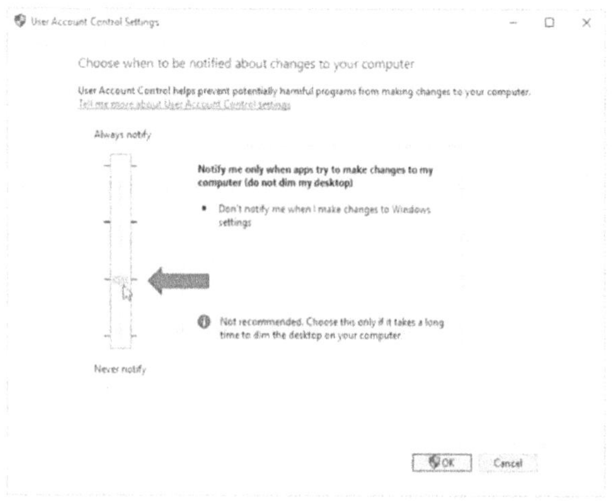

# Windows Defender

Windows Defender is another security tools from Windows. The Windows Defender is both a malware protection tool and an antivirus that is built into your operating system. This tools scan your computer to detect malicious software, it also check each program or file you open for malwares.

The steps below will help you to configure Windows Defender.

**Step 1** – Go to **SETTINGS** and Choose **Update & security**.

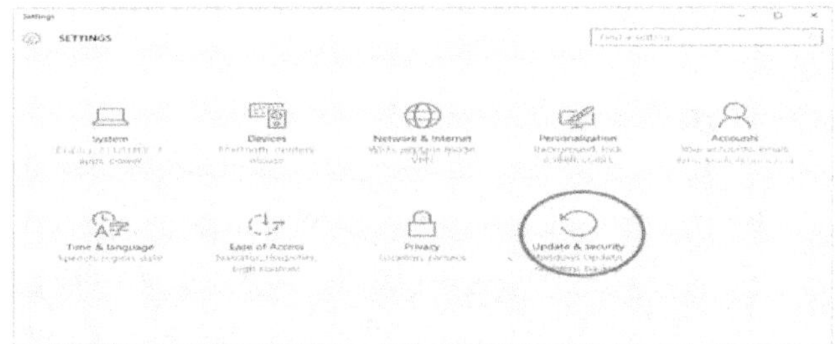

**Step 2** – In the **UPDATE & SECURITY** window, choose **Windows Defender**.

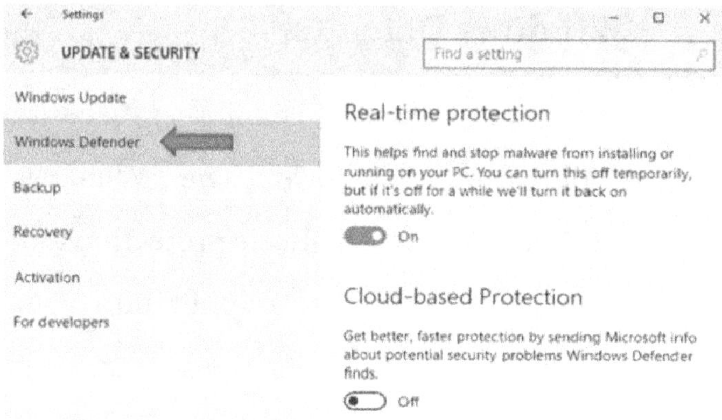


In this window, you can customize your settings such as activating cloud-based protection, this enables Windows Defender to send information about the security threats it finds on your system to Microsoft. You can also turn off real-time protection here.

## Windows Firewall

Windows Firewall prohibits unauthorized access to your computer from the outside. By default, it is activated to defend your network and computer.

The steps below will help you to customize your Firewall-

**Step 1** – Open the **Control Panel** you can search for it via the search bar

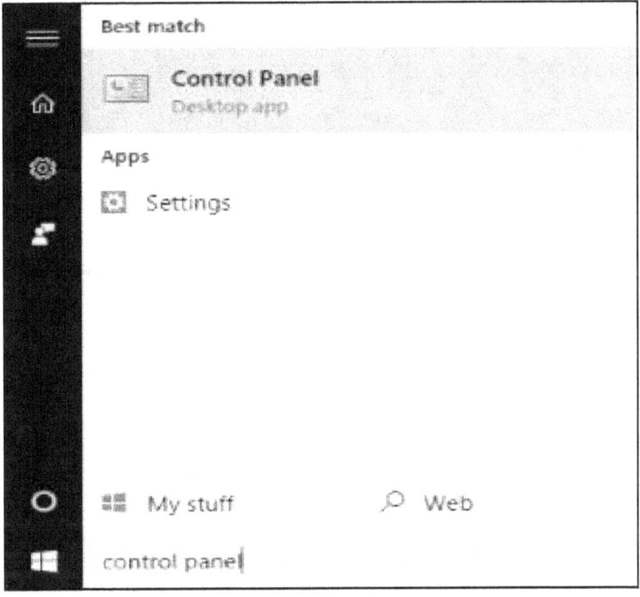


**Step 2** – After the Control Panel is open, select **Windows Firewall**.

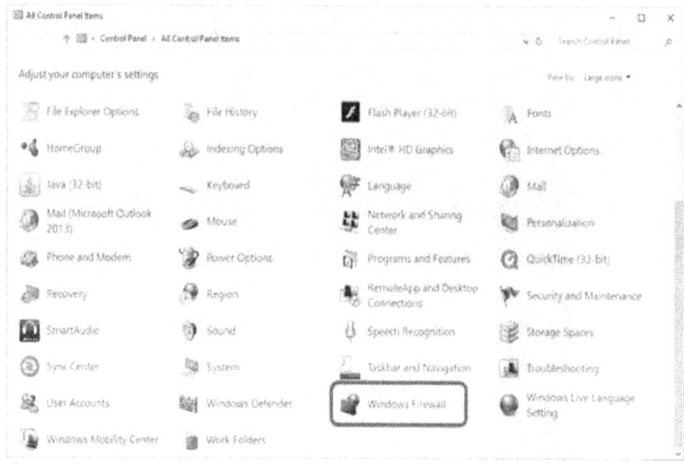

**Step 3** – when you open the **Windows Firewall** window, you can customize the settings either by turning it on or off or selecting when to safeguard your computer

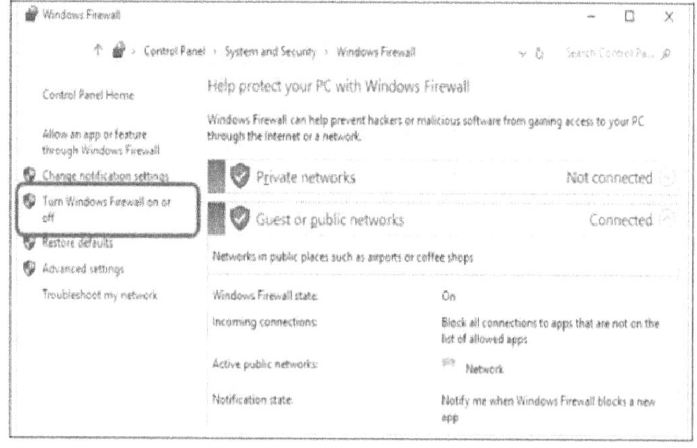

# Chapter 16

# Parental Control

Windows 10 gives you the opportunity to create a child's account for your kids. With a kid's account, you can put restrictions in place and monitor the activities of your children on a computer.

The steps below will guide you to set up a child's account –

**Step 1** – Go to **SETTINGS** and select **Accounts**.

**Step 2** – In the **ACCOUNTS** window, choose the option "**Family & other users**".

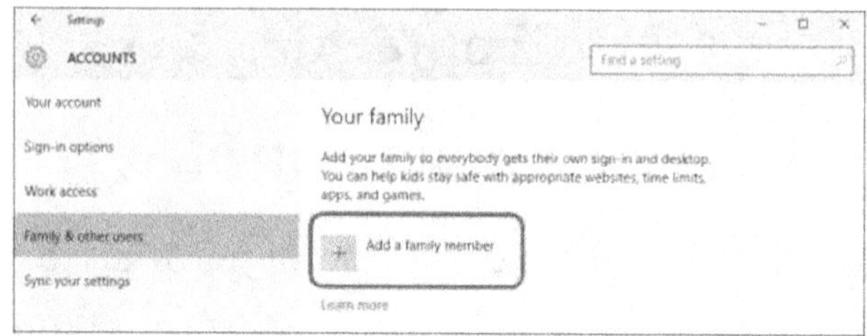

**Step 3** – Select the "Add a family member.

**Step 4** – Select the family member you wish to add (an adult or a child)

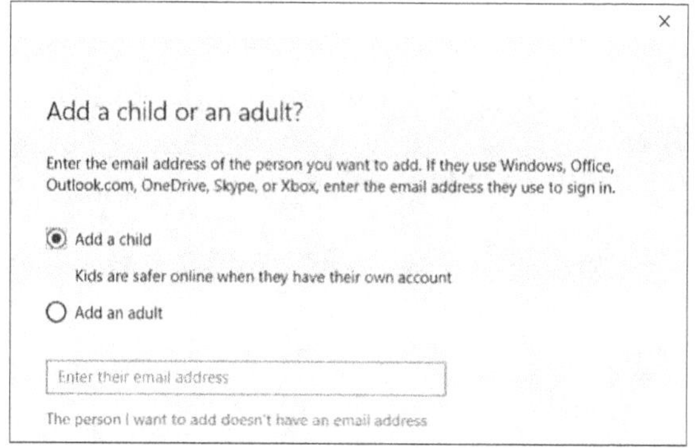


**Step 5** – Next you will be will be asked to set up an account for your child. If they do not have an e-mail account, go ahead to open an Outlook account for them.

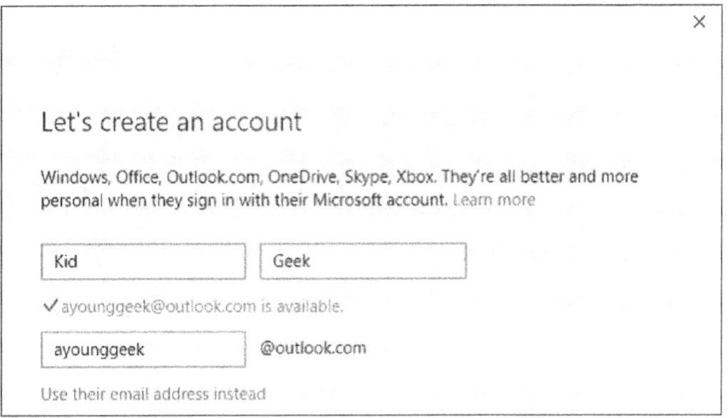



**Step 6** – Add a phone number to the account for security. This will be used to retrieve the account if it became inaccessible or the account got hacked.

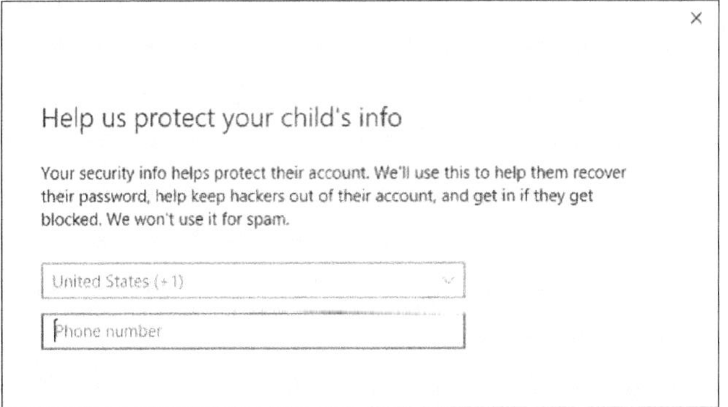



**Step 7** – select from notification and experience preferences, for example, if you want Microsoft to send you promotional offers.

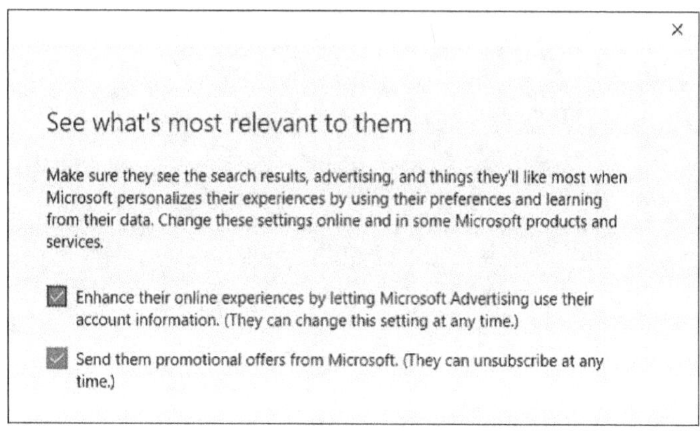



Once the account is created your kid(s) are free to log in their customized windows 10 account.

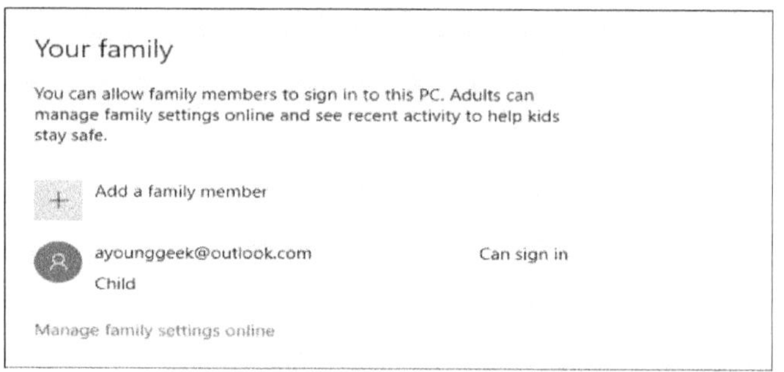



Furthermore, you can choose to supervise the activities of your kid(s) in the account by turning on the option to report his activity.

You can as well decide to block "unsuitable websites" to confine your child's browsing to only acceptable websites.

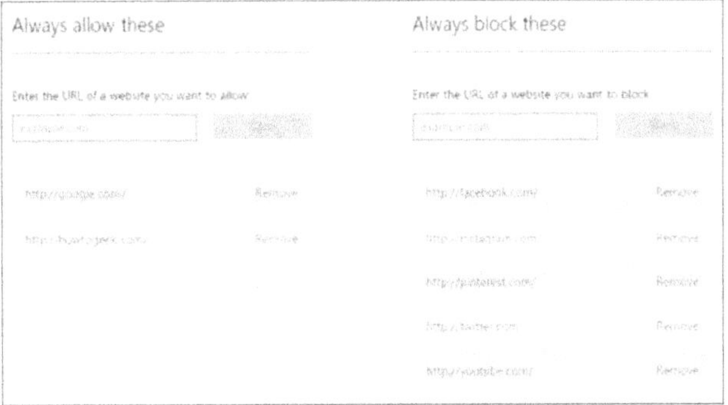

In conclusion, you can equally determine when your kid (s) is permitted to log in by creating a schedule.

Choose the times Kid Geek can use devices

|  | As early as | No later than | Limit per day, on this device |
|---|---|---|---|
| Sunday | 7:00 AM | 9:00 PM | 4 hrs |
| Monday | 7:00 AM | 9:00 PM | 2 hrs |
| Tuesday | 7:00 AM | 9:00 PM | 2 hrs |
| Wednesday | 7:00 AM | 9:00 PM | 2 hrs |
| Thursday | 7:00 AM | 9:00 PM | 2 hrs |
| Friday | 7:00 AM | 11:00 PM | 4 hrs |
| Saturday | 7:00 AM | 11:00 PM | 4 hrs |

# Chapter 17

# Applications

In Windows 10, there are several ways you can access your applications. The easiest is to use the search box in the taskbar to search for the application's name.

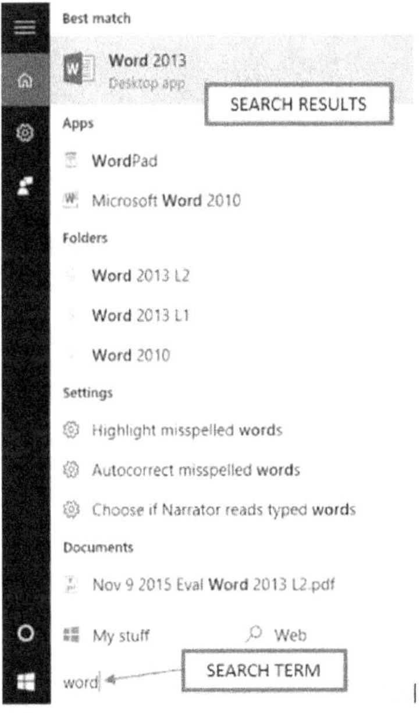


One other simple option is to go to your start menu and select **All Apps**

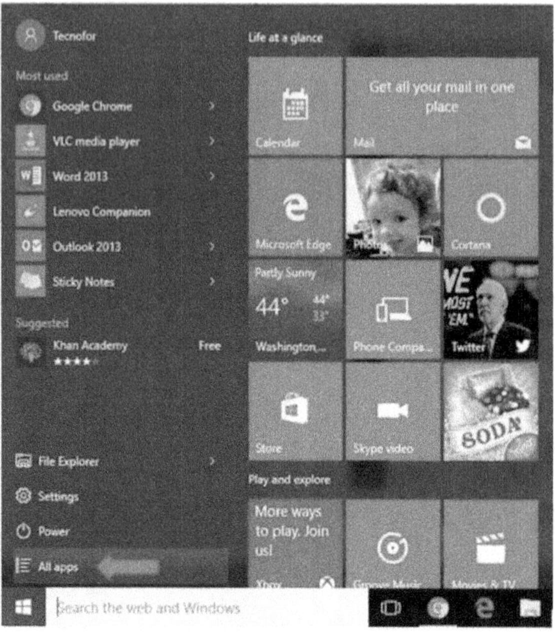



When you select All Apps, Windows 10 will bring out a list of all the applications you have installed in your computer in an alphabetical order.

0 – 9
3D Builder
A
Absolute Software
Acrobat Reader DC
Alarms & Clock
Apple Software Update
AVAST Software
C
Calculator
Calendar
Camera
Candy Crush Soda Saga
Conexant
Contact Support
Cortana
G
Back
Life at a glance
We speak Outlook
Calendar
Mail
Microsoft Edge
Photo
Cortana
Partly Sunny
44°
44°
33°
Washington,...
Phone Compa...
Twitter
Store
Skype video
Play and explore
Xbox
Groove Music
Movies & TV
Search the web and Windows

# Chapter 18

# Web Browsing

Windows 10 comes pre-built with the Edge Browser, the advanced new browser from Microsoft. You can automatically accessed the Edge browser by its icon located on the taskbar.

The Edge Windows is similar to what you get in most modern web browsers

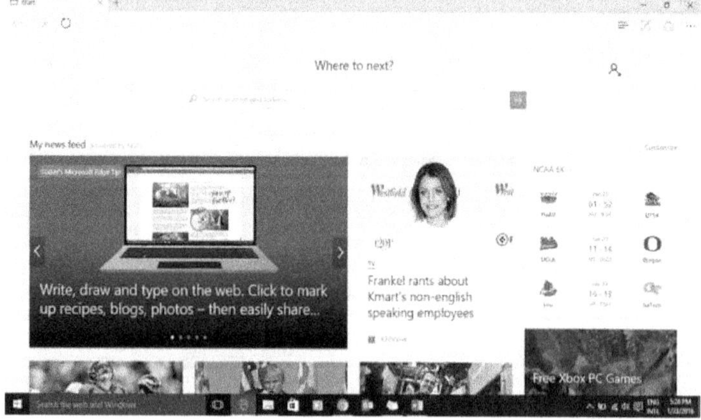

However, the toolbar of the Edge Browser is easier than that of Internet Explorer.

You will find the following buttons -

1. **Back** – accesses the previous web page.

2. **Forward** – accesses the next web page.

3. **Refresh** – Reloads your web page.

4. **New tab** – Add additional tab to access a different web page.

5. **Hub (Favorites and History)** – access your favorite lists, favorite web sites and history of websites visited.

6. **Web Notes** – Make Web Notes on the web page.

7. **Share** – Share the web page through e-mail or other methods.

8. **More options** – access more options to configure the browser.

# Reviewing Browsing History

The "Hub" button can also give you a "History" or list of websites you've visited.

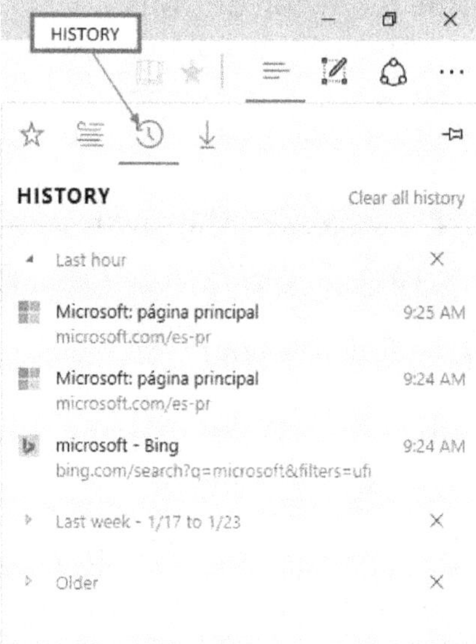



The Clear all history" options allows you to

clear the history of your visited webpages

If you so desired

# Chapter 19

# Networking

Just like earlier Windows versions, you can get to know your network connection status in your Windows 10 notification area.

If you are on a wireless connection, the icon below will be display

If you are on a wired connection, the icon below will appear.

# Wired Connection (Ethernet)

If the source of your network connection is cable, you can open its settings from the **SETTINGS** window, and choosing Network **& Internet**.

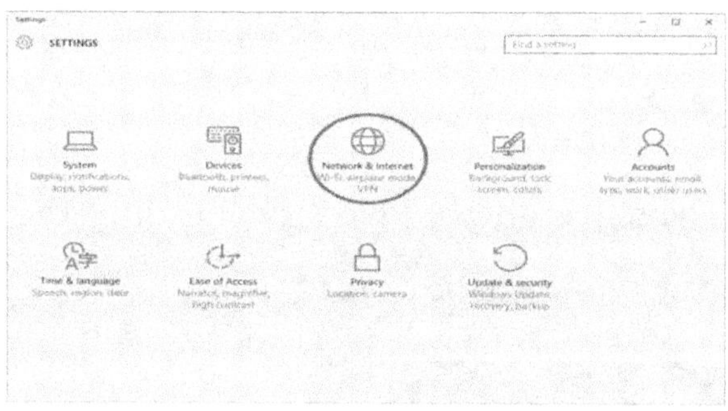

When you open **NETWORK & INTERNET** window, select **Ethernet** to access the settings of your connection.

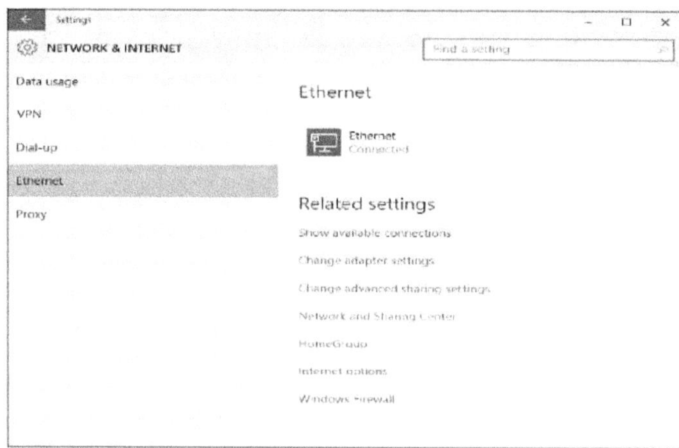

# Wireless Connection (Wi-Fi)

If you are using a wireless connection, a click of the wireless icon will display information about your connection and other available wireless networks.

A click on **Network settings** will allow you to access the Network & Internet window, which provides more precise information about your connection, and available configuration options.

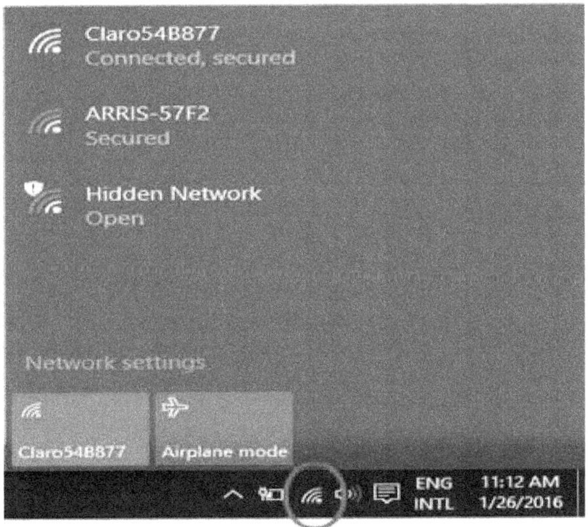

You can turn on or off your **WIRESS NETWORK CONNECTION** In the Network &Internet Window.

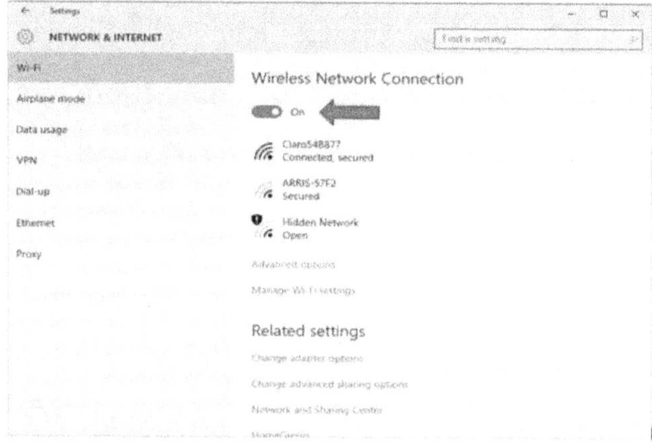

# Chapter 20

# Virtualization

One unique feature introduced to Windows 10 OS is the ability to create virtual machines. In its simplest meaning, a virtual machine is a software emulation of a computer (system). Virtual machines are created within a physical or real computer, enabling you to create many separate computers which have the capacity to run different programs and operating systems. Virtual machines are control with the use of a special software known as a **Hypervisor.** The software for Microsoft's virtual machine is called Hyper-V

Because Virtualization is a really advanced process, only some selected computers can run virtual machines. Before now, only servers have the capacity to do this.

However, with the introduction of advanced operating systems such as Windows 10, everyone can now create their own virtual machines.

Requirements in Windows 10

In Windows 10, the following constitutes the basic requirements for creating and running virtual machines

- A 64-bit version of Windows 10 Pro or Windows Enterprise. Hyper-V **cannot be operated on Windows 10 Home edition**.

- A computer processor that support virtualization, or more explicitly SLAT (Secondary Level Address Translation).

- Virtualization must be enabled in your computer's BIOS. The BIOS is a small program that controls the boot-up of your computer ensuring that everything is working perfectly fine.

## What version of Windows do you have?

To know the specific Window version of your computer, observe the steps below-

**Step 1** – go to the **Control Panel** by typing it in through the Search bar.

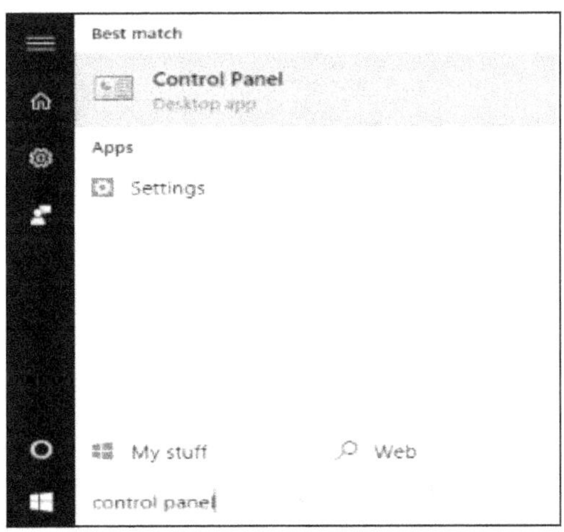


**Step 2** – in the control panel window select **System**.

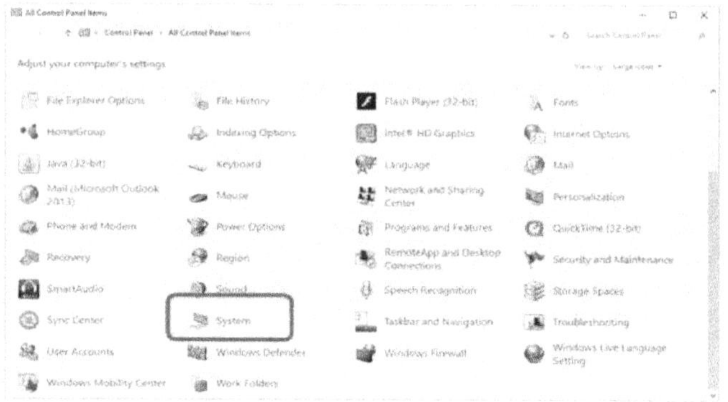

**Step 3** – when you open the **System** window you can see the particular version of windows and the type of processor of your computer

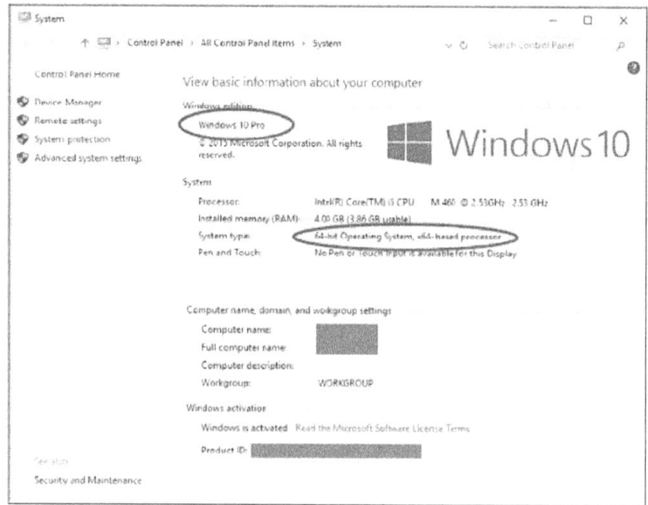

## Enabling Virtualization in the BIOS

As stated earlier, the BIOS is a small program that runs anytime you power on your computer. Its function is to help the computer's boot up process by ensuring that everything is working smoothly. But it equally controls some advanced functions in your computer, and they need to be enabled to become functional, **Virtualization** is one of these functions.

The following steps will help you enable Virtualization in your computer-

**Step 1** – Restart your PC and open the BIOS setup. To enter the setup, just press a key as the computer is turned on. The specific key you will press differs from one computer to another, however, it usually is the Delete, F2, or F10. Most computers tell you the specific key to press to enter the setup, or you can check the manual of your computer.

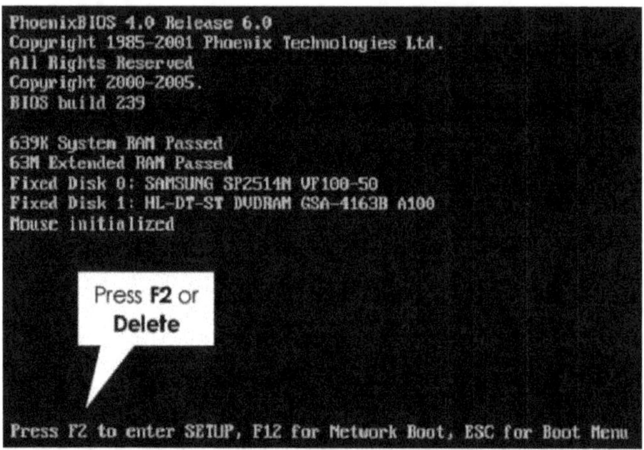



**Step 2** – After you have entered the BIOS setup, you have to enable all virtualization settings. The BIOS equally differs greatly from one computer to another, depending on the brand.

```
                    Phoenix TrustedCore(tm) Setup Utility
        Advanced

    Advanced Processor Configuration              Item Specific Help

 CPU Mismatch Detection:          [Enabled]     When enabled, a VMM
 Core Multi-Processing:           [Enabled]     (Virtual Machine
 Processor Power Management:      [Disabled]    Monitor) can utilize
 Intel(R) Virtualization Technology [Enabled]   the additional hardware
 Execute Disable Bit:             [Enabled]     capabilities provided
                                                by Vanderpool
 Adjacent Cache Line Prefetch:    [Disabled]    Technology.
 Hardware Prefetch:               [Disabled]
 Direct Cache Access              [Disabled]    If this option is
                                                changed, a Power Off-On
                                                sequence will be
 Set Max Ext CPUID = 3            [Disabled]    applied on the next
                                                boot.

 F1   Info   ↑↓  Select Item   -/+  Change Values    F9   Setup Defaults
 Esc  Exit   ←   Select Menu  Enter Select ▶ Sub-Menu F10  Save and Exit
```

**Step 3** – Once you have enabled all necessary settings, save and exit the BIOS setup. You can do this by pressing F10. Your computer will restart after this.

# Setting Up Hyper-V

In order to create and control Virtual machines, you have to set up Hyper-V from Microsoft. The following steps will help you to do this -

**Step 1** – go to the **Control Panel**

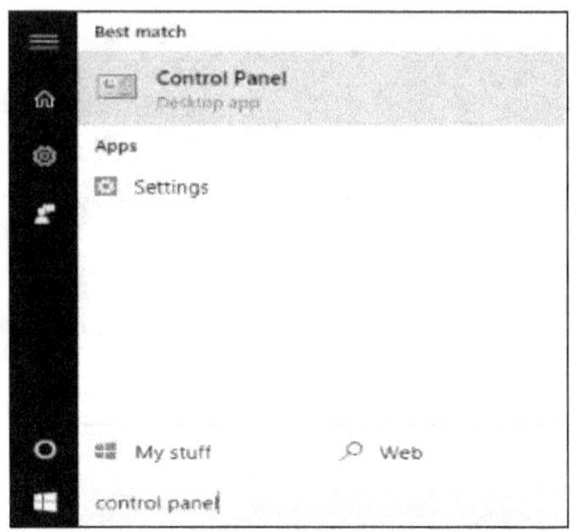

**Step 2** – After opening the Control Panel window, select **Programs and Features**.

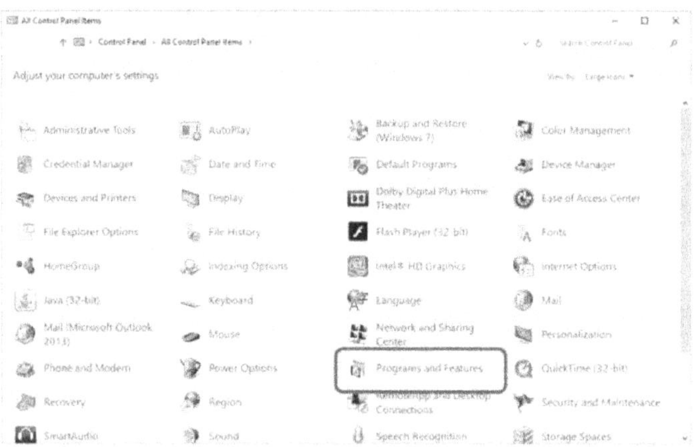

**Step 3** – when you open **Programs and Features** window, select "Turn Windows features on or off".

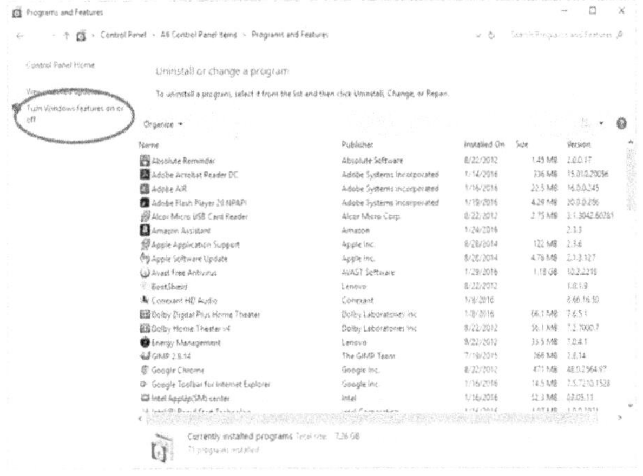

## Step 4 – In the **Windows Features** window, search for the Hyper-V functionality and tick all the boxes.

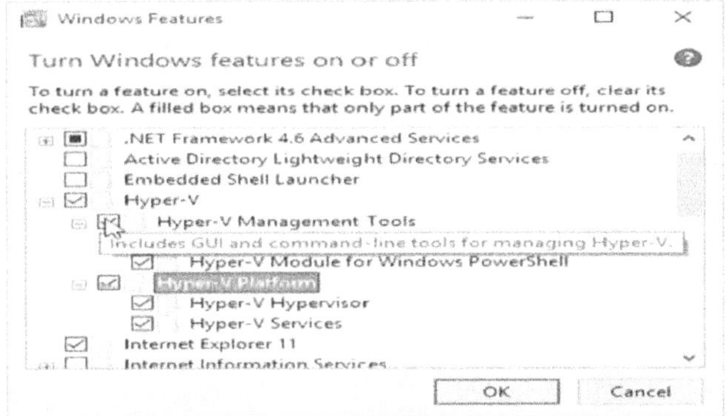


After this, Windows will install and configure Hyper-V, then it will ask you to restart and confirm the changes. Once you do that, it will then go through a succession of restarts to finish configuration of your computer

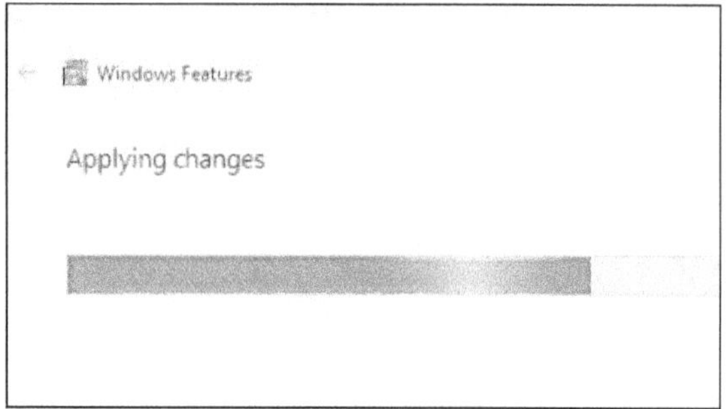


# Creating a Virtual Machine with Hyper-V

After successful installation of Hyper-V in your windows 10 computer, you can open it and use it to create virtual machines. To start Hyper-V and to use it to create a virtual machine, observe the following steps–

**Step** 1 – Go to Control Panel and choose **Administrative Tools**.

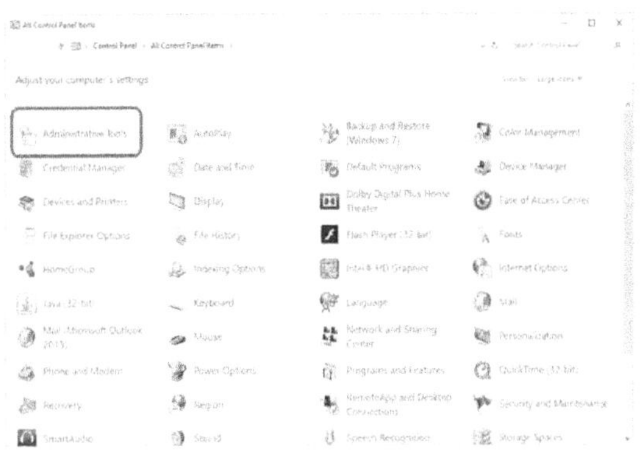

## Step 2 – In the **Administrative Tools** window, select **Hyper-V Manager**.

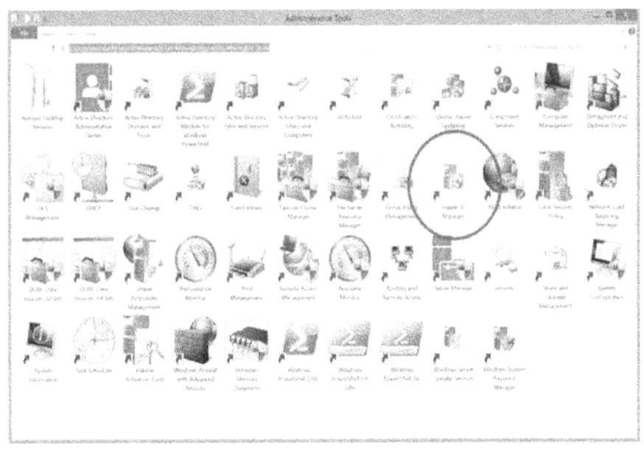

## Step 3 – As soon as Hyper-V starts running, you will see the name of your computer system on below the Hyper-V manager. Choose the computer to work on it.

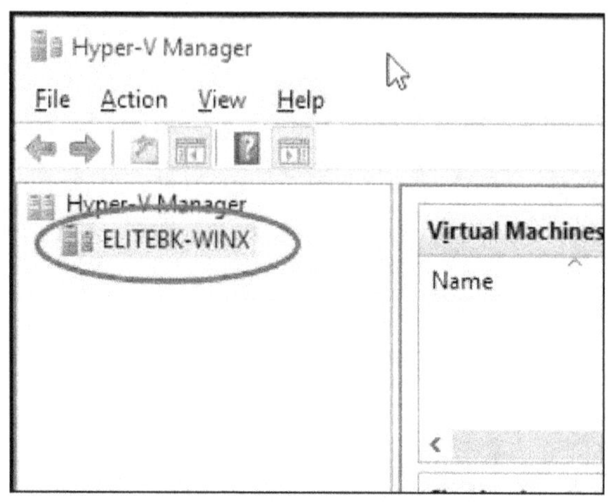

**Step 4** – Go to the **Action** menu,

click **New** and **Virtual Machine**.

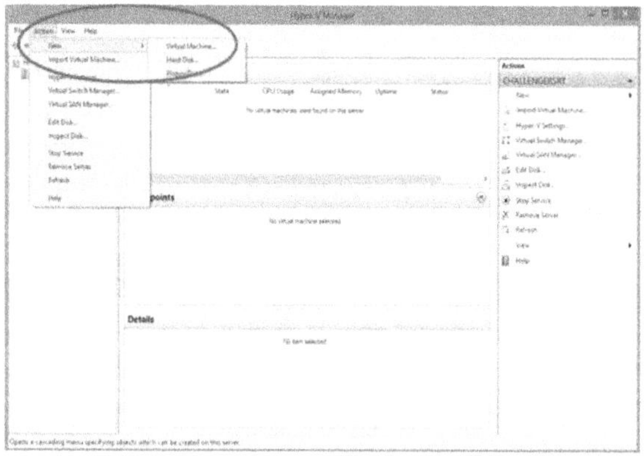

This can also be performed from the sidebar, under the Actions tab on the right side of your applications.

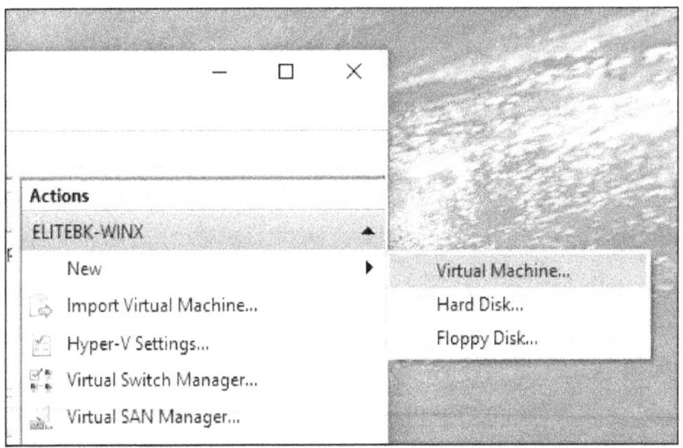


**Step 5** – Next, Hyper-V will open the **New Virtual Machine Wizard** to assist you in creating a virtual machine. You can click finish at this point to create a virtual machine that has some simple configurations, or if you are an advanced user, you can click next to create a customized virtual machine for yourself.

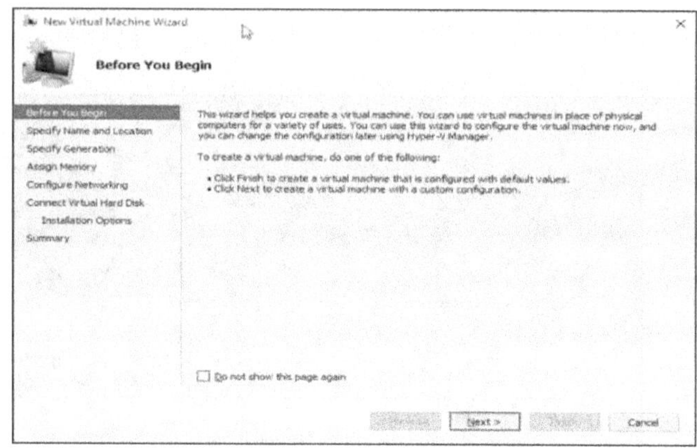

**Step 6** – After you have successfully created the virtual machine, you will see it in the Hyper-V window.

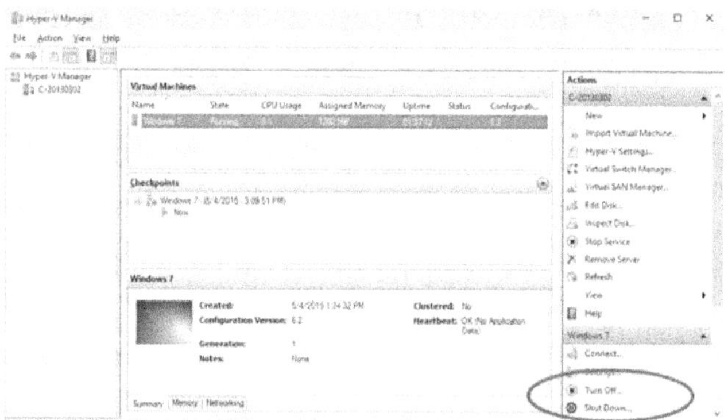

Just like physical computers that you can touch, virtual machines must have an operating system installed on them in order to function. Hyper-V allows enables you to turn them on or shut them down with the help of the buttons located at the far right.

# Chapter 21

# Remote Access

Remote Desktop is one feature in your computer that enables you to access a different computer from your own computer system from a remote location.

## Enabling Remote Access to your Computer

In order to use Remote Access, you have to first configure the remote computer to accept connections from remote locations. The setting for this cis automatically turned off in your system to prevent unwanted connections. The steps below will help you to turn on your remote connection.

# Step 1 – Go to the **Control Panel**

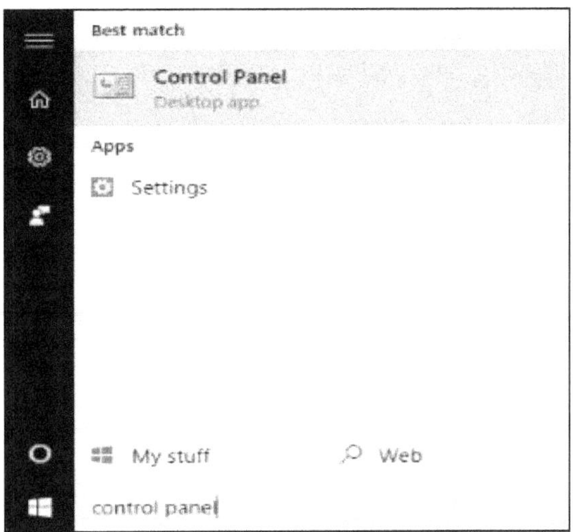

## Step 2 – After opening the Control Panel window, choose **System**.

**Step 3** – when you open the System window, note the "Computer Name"; you are going to need it later on.

**Step 4** – after that, select the link "Change settings" to open the **System Properties** window.

**Step 5** – when you open the System Properties window, you can check the "Computer Name" once more, and then choose the **Remote** tab.

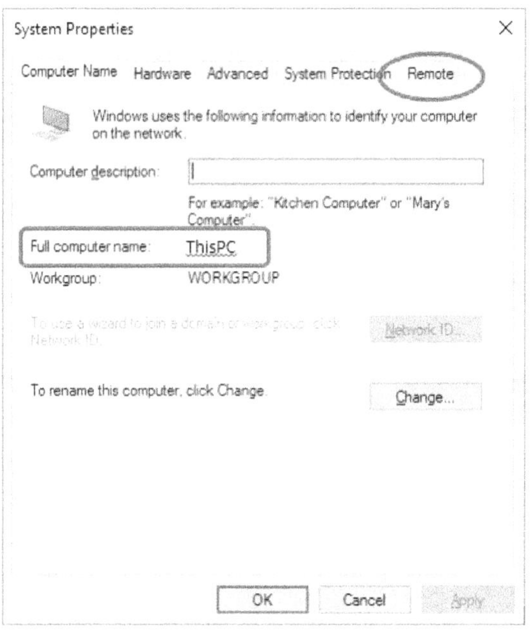

**Step 6** – when the Remote tab is opened, choose the option that reads "Allow Remote connection to this computer".

**Step 7** – once you choose the appropriate option, ensure sure you click **OK** or **Apply** to save your changes. This will ensure other people can access your computer system from remote locations.

## Use Remote Desktop to access another Computer

Having enabled remove connections on your system, the following steps will help you access your computer remotely.

**Step 1** – Go to the **Remote Desktop Connection** window, you can search for this via the Taskbar.

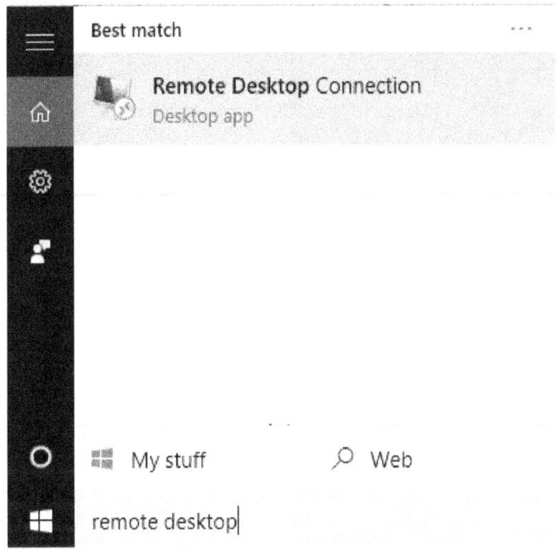


**Step 2** – when the Remote Desktop Connection window is open, type the name of the computer you wish to access and select **Connect**.

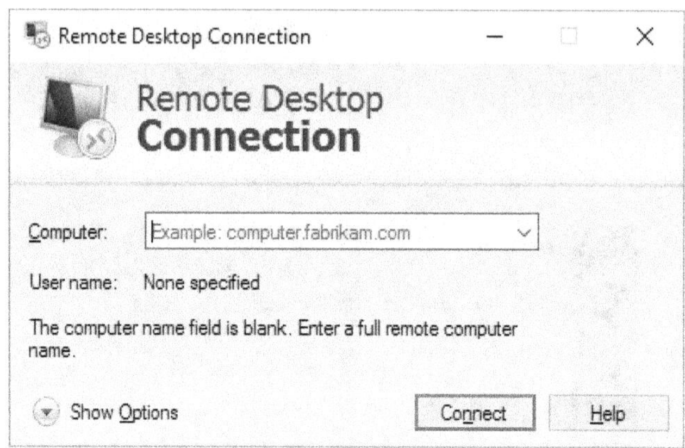

**Step 3** – Once you are able to connect, the Desktop of the remote computer will appear on your system, and you can work on it.

# Chapter 22

# Backup & Recovery

There are several tools in Windows 10 that will help you back up your files and documents. Some of them are discussed below.

## File History

File History will back-up the files located in your library sections (Pictures, Documents, Music, etc.). File history allows you to select a specific drive to back-up your files and then asks you the time to do it.

Follow these steps to configure your File History backup –

**Step 1** – Open **SETTINGS** and click **Update & security**.

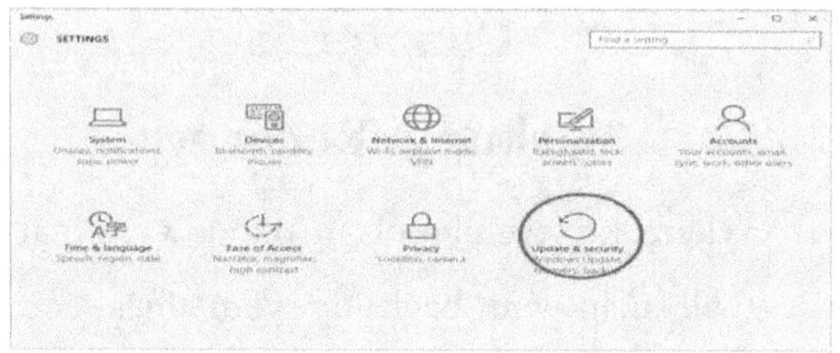

## Step 2 –when the UPDATE & SECURITY window opens, select Backup.

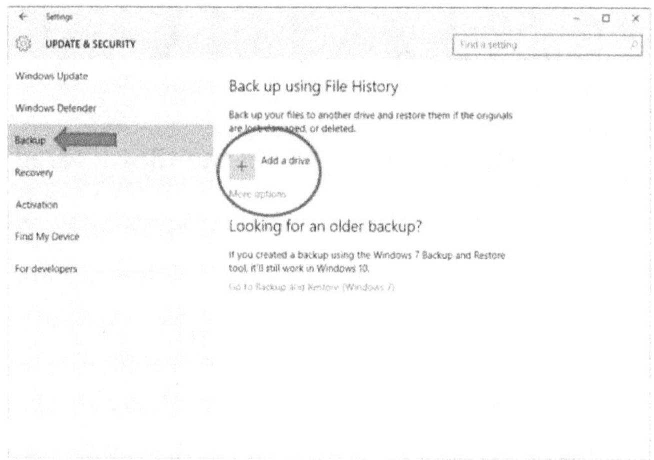

## Step 3 – Choose "Add a drive" to select where to store your backup.

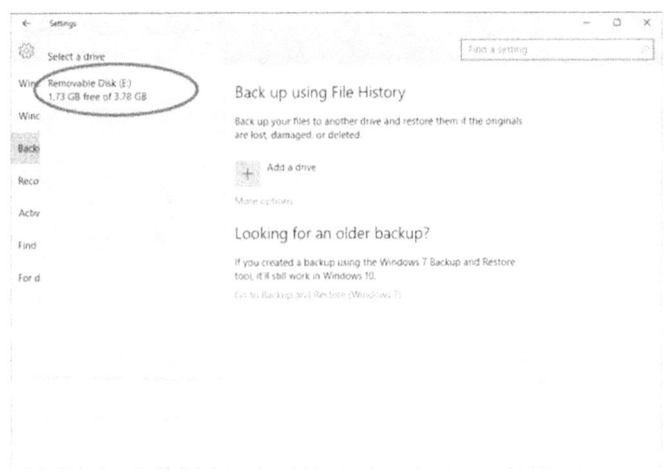

# Backup & Restore (Windows 7)

The backup & restore tool was removed in Windows 8 and 8.1, but has been re-introduced in Windows 10. This tool allows you to perform back-ups and restore data from old Windows 7 backups.in addition, it also allows you to back-up your documents regularly on Windows 10.

To access the Back-up & Restore function, the following steps will help you- **Step**

1 – Go to the **Control Panel** you can access it through the Search bar.

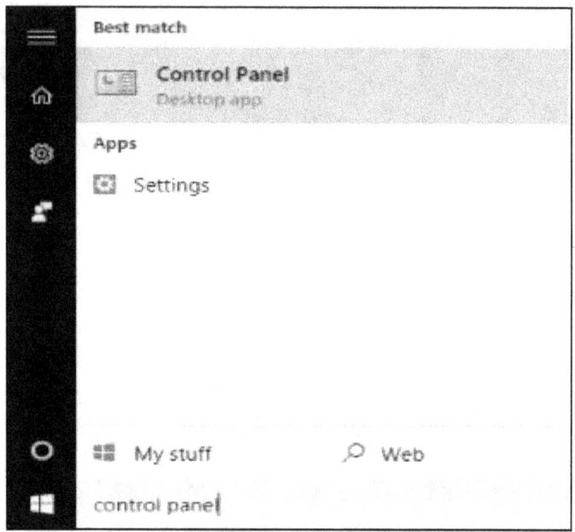


**Step 2** – After you open the Control Panel window, select **Backup and Restore (Windows 7)**.

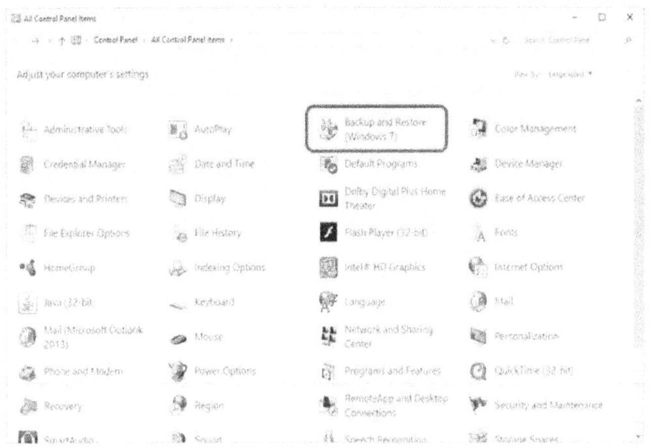

**Step 3** – when you open the Backup & Restore window, choose to "Set up backup".

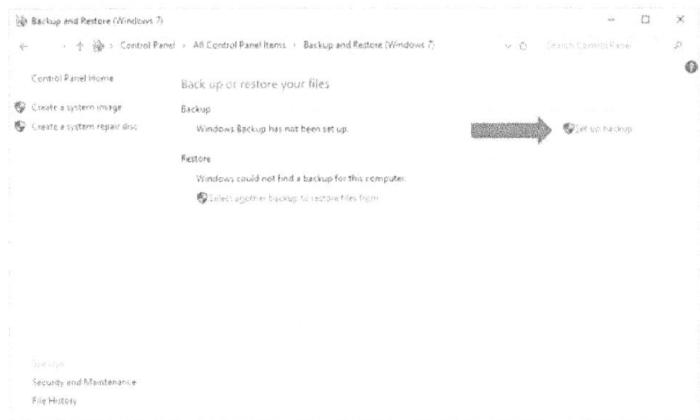

**Step 4** – when you open the **Set up backup** window, select the specific storage you want to have your backup stored.

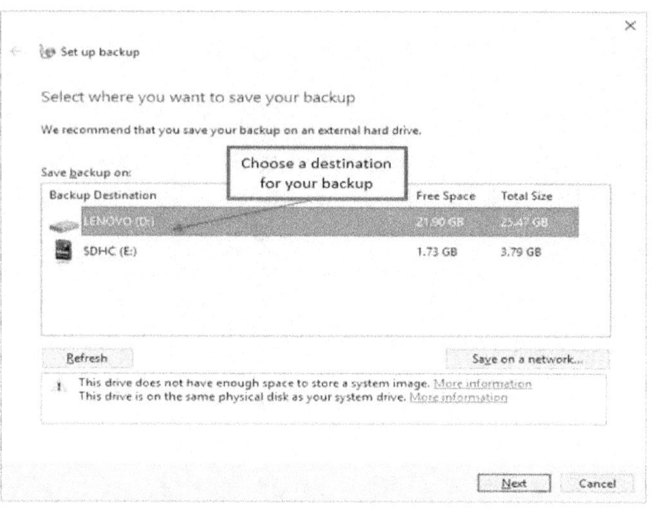


When choosing any of the listed storage
devices, Windows 10 will provide you with
information about that particular device.
When you have selected the destination
you want to have your backup files saved,
click **Next**.

**Step 5** – when the next window opened, you can select the files you want to backup.

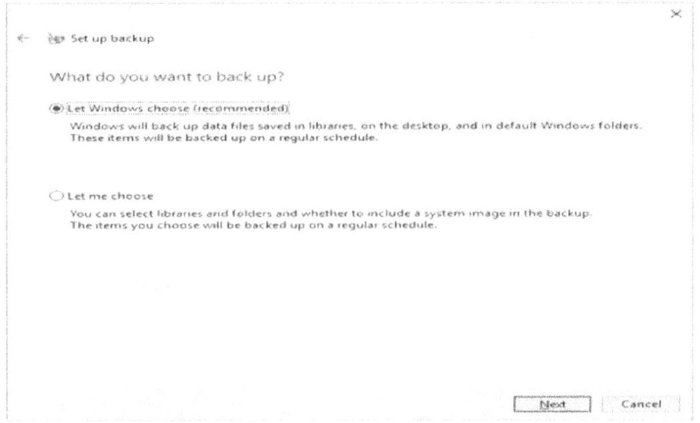


By default, Windows is configured to store everything in your libraries (Pictures Documents, Music, etc.) and in your Desktop, however, you can equally choose particular folders and files to backup. Once you have selected the files, click **Next**.

**Step 6** – when you open next which coincidentally is the last window, you can review the settings of your backup and create the schedule when you want to have it perform.

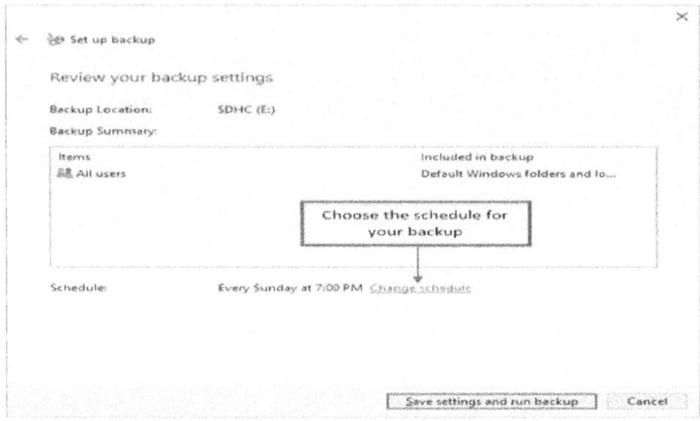



**Step 7** –finally, select **Save settings and run backup**. Your back up will be carry out at the exact time you scheduled.

## Creating a System Image

If you experience a system failure, Windows 10 provides you some options to restore it to a particular state. System Image is one of these options. A system image is copy of everything on your computer and program files necessary for smooth running of your computer.

You can apply this alternative to store a copy of your computer at a particular time, and later on, you can have your computer restore to that specific state. The options to do this is located in the Backup and Restore window we talk about earlier.

**Step 1** – from the control panel open the **Backup and Restore** window

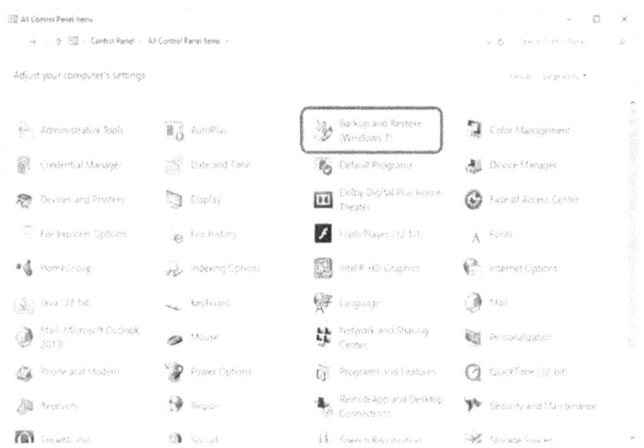

**Step 2** –when the **Backup and Restore** window opens, select the "Create a system image" selection.

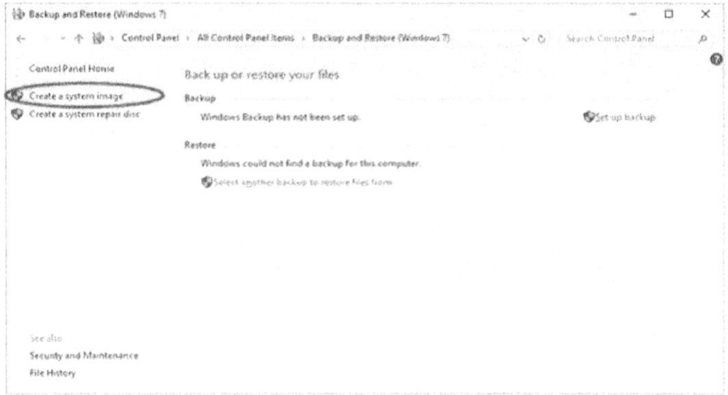

**Step 3** – when you open the **Create a system image** window, choose where to store the backup from among three alternatives: on DVD's, on your hard disk, or in the network.

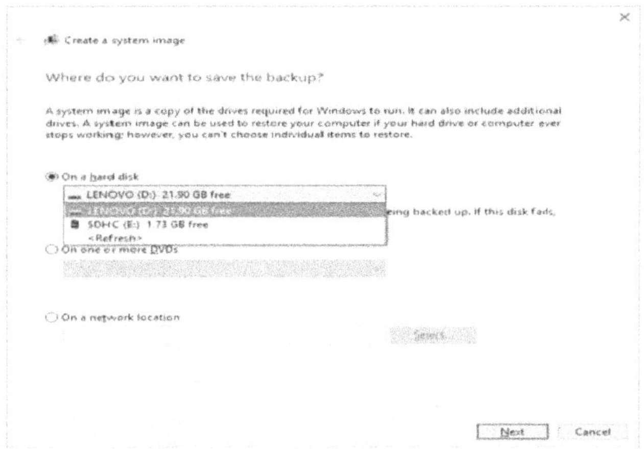

Click Next after you selected where to store the backup.

**Step 4** – confirm your image settings in the next window, and click **Start backup**.

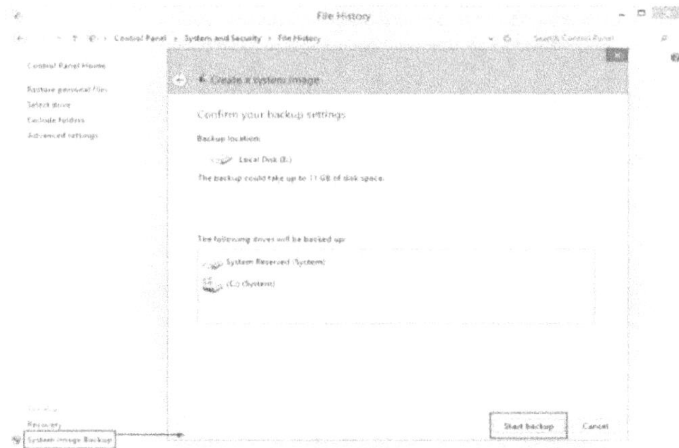

## Resetting the PC

One other option provided by Windows 10 for system recovery is called "Reset this PC". This system recovery option enables you to return your computer to its original factory settings. It equally offers you the choice of keeping your files or removing all your files. Follow these steps reset your PC

**Step 1** – Open **SETTINGS** and choose Update **& security**.

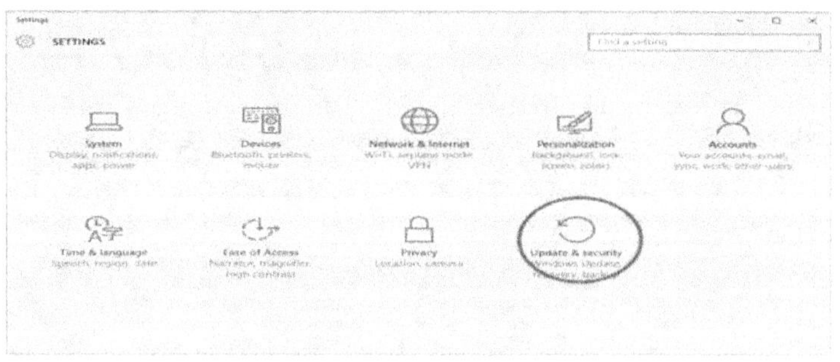

**Step 2** – Choose **Recovery** when you open the update and security window

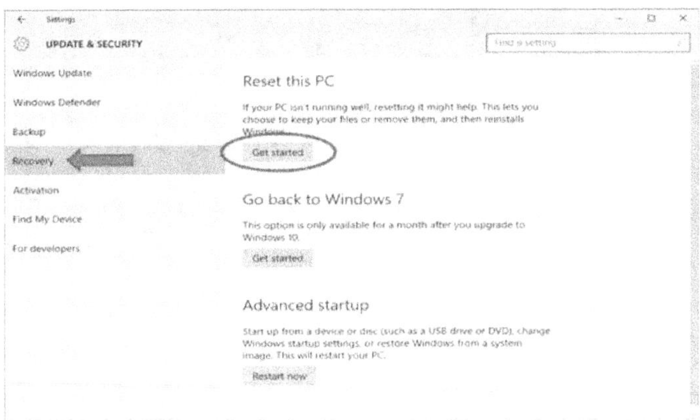

**Step 3** – when you open the **Recovery** window, you can select the "Get started" button. You will find this button under "reset this PC"

**Step 4** – in the next window, will ask be asked whether you wish to reset your settings and applications, and still keep your personal files, or simply remove everything and return your computer to its original state.

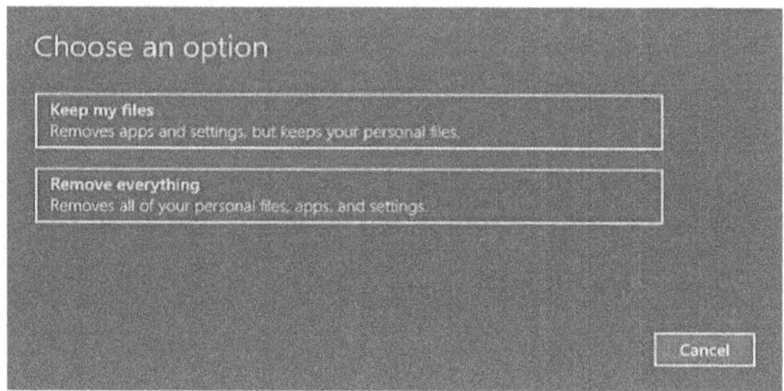


## Advanced Options

In Windows 10, there are several advanced options available to restore your PC. Even though these are developed for advanced Windows users, you can gain access to them from the same **Update & Security** window we discussed earlier.

**Step 1** –Go to the **Settings** window and choose **UPDATE & SECURITY**.

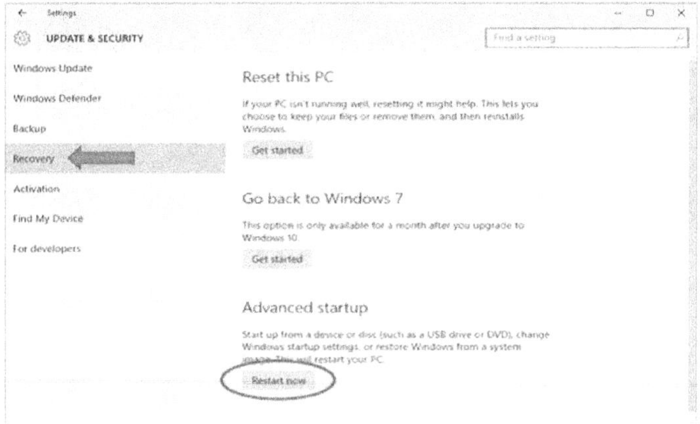

**Step 2 –** When the **UPDATE & SECURITY** window opens, choose **Recovery.** Next, click the **Restart** now button located under advanced startup

**Step 3** – Windows 10 will give you different options to choose from when it restarts.

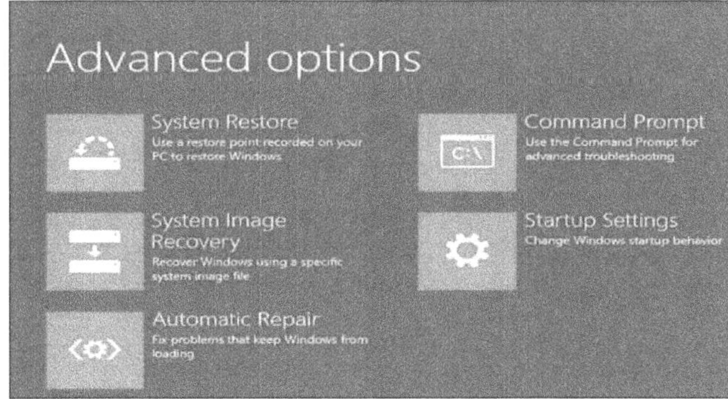

You see this same menu whenever
Windows whenever Windows experience
booting failure.

# Chapter 23

# Apps Management

With Windows 10 OS, you have numerous ways to access your applications. And as we pointed out earlier, one of the simplest ways to do this is to click **ALL APPS** in the search menu.

When you do this, it will show all the applications installed in your computer in an alphabetical order. If you have a recently installed application, it will be named "New"

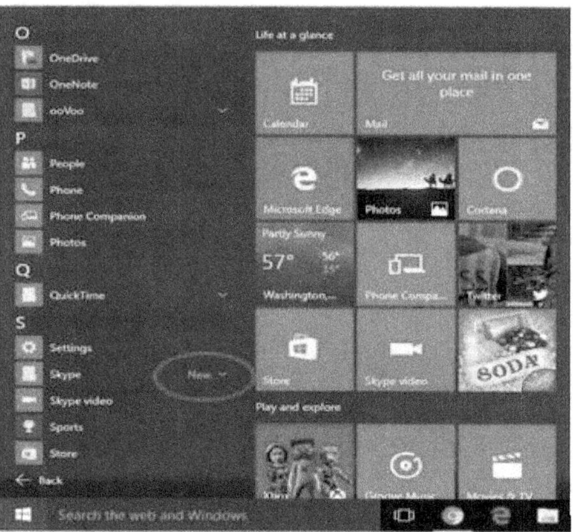

**Uninstalling Applications**

If you want to remove or uninstalled an unwanted application, there are three major ways you can do this -

- From the Start Menu

- From the Settings window

- From the Control Panel

The steps to uninstall your applications using each of the methods are explained below.

**Uninstalling an Application from the Start Menu**

Uninstalling application from the start menu is probably the easiest method uninstalling an app. To do this take the following steps –

**Step 1** – Go to the Start Menu and select **All Apps**.

**Step 2** – look for the application you wish to uninstall from the displayed list, and right-click it

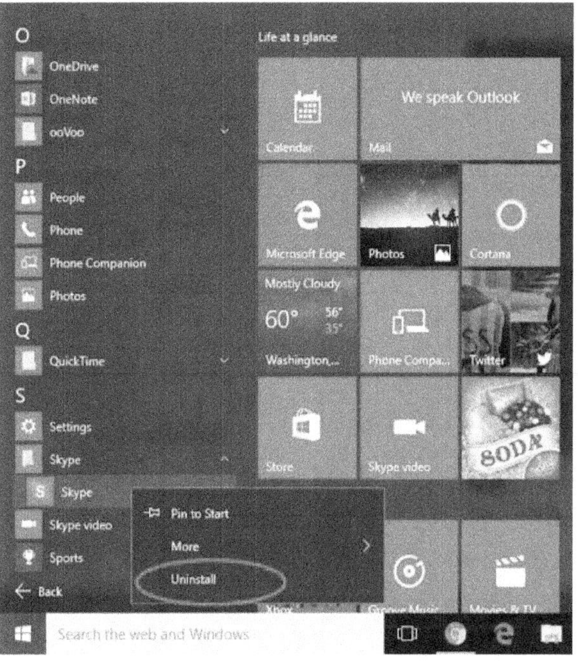

**Step 3** – Choose **Uninstall**. Then follow the steps necessary to complete the process. The steps are different for each application.

## Uninstalling an Application from the Settings window

Uninstalling application through the Settings Window is a new method of removing unwanted applications. To do this, take the following steps-

**Step 1** – Go to the Start Menu and choose **Settings**.

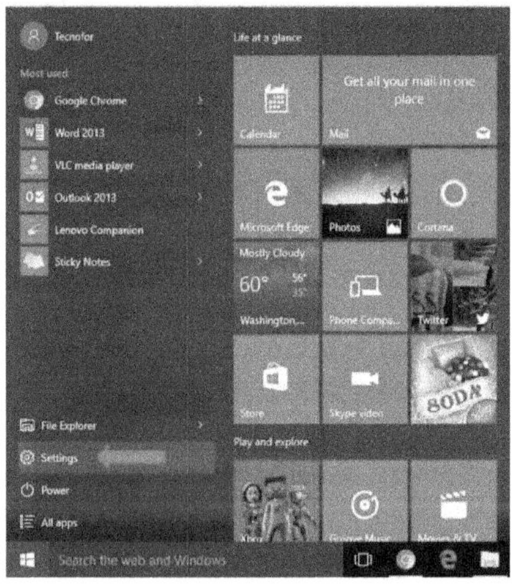

**Step 2** – Next choose **SYSTEM** on the settings window

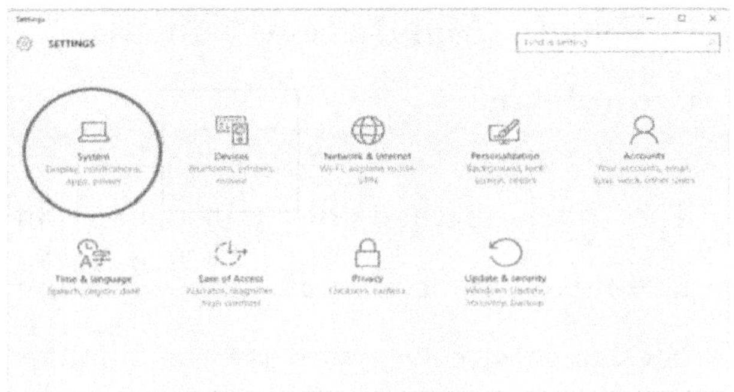

## Step 3 – Next choose **Apps & features**.

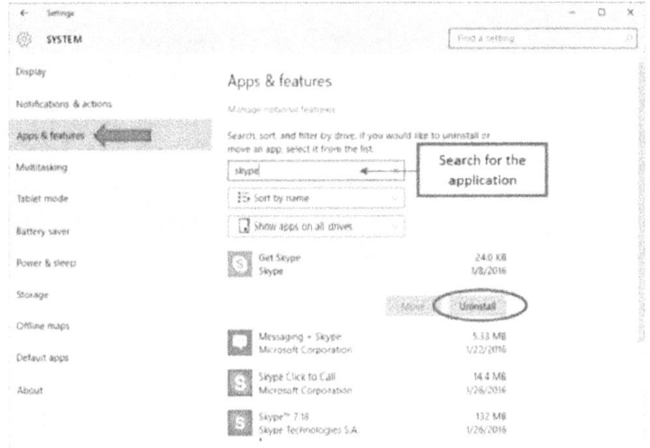


## Step 4 – Next search for the app you wish to uninstall in the search box on the **Apps & features** window.

## Step 5 – finally from the results, select on the application and click **Uninstall**.

## Uninstalling Applications from the Control Panel

The final method of uninstalling an unwanted application is more common because it involves the use the popular control panel. To uninstall an application with this method, follow these steps –

**Step 1** – Go to the **Control Panel**

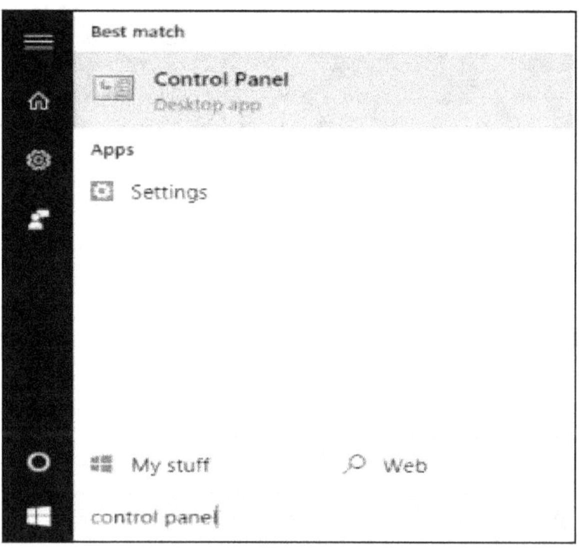



**Step 2** – Next choose **Programs and Features**

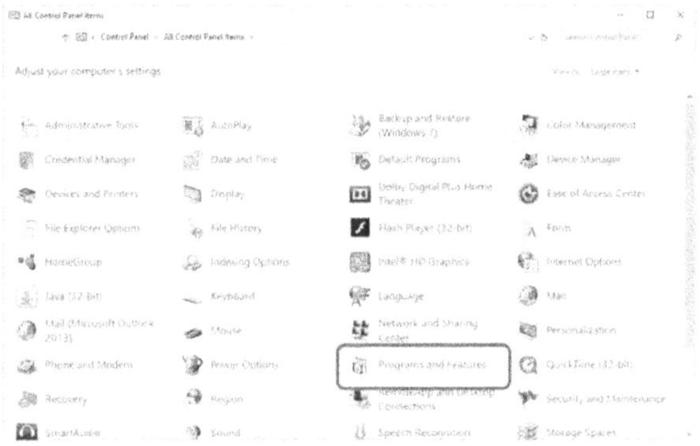

**Step 3** – when the **Programs and Features** window is open, it will display a list of every application you have installed on your system. To uninstall any application, simply click the application and click the uninstall button.

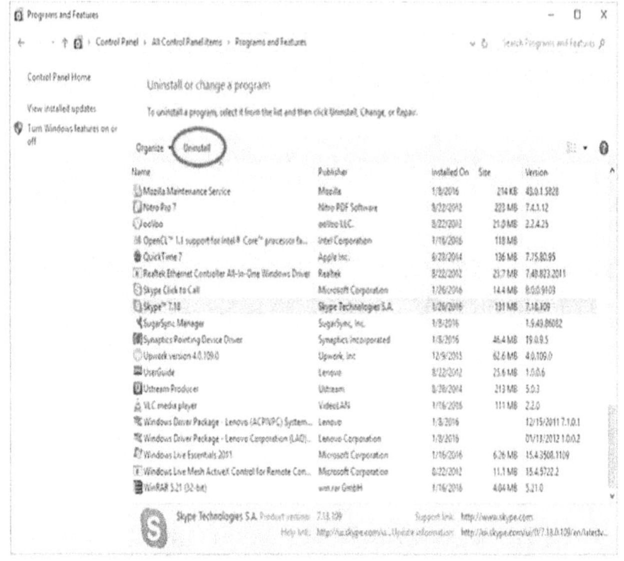

Another method you can do this is by right-clicking the application on the list.

In this window, you can also get additional information about the applications installed on your computer such as -

- The date it was installed.

- The size it occupies on your hard disk.

- The particular version of the application

# Chapter 24

# Email Management

The new **Mail** app is integrated into Windows 10 to help you handle your e-mails. The Mail app can be accessed directly from the Start Menu.

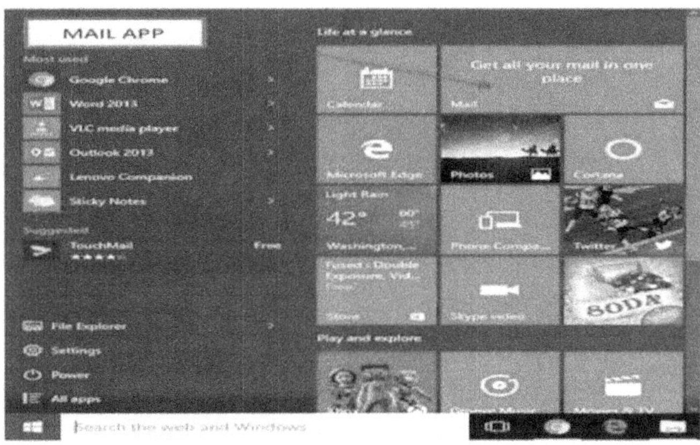

If your mail account is connected to Windows, the Mail app will by default configure itself to give you access to your e-mails. However, the Mail app will ask you to do the configuration yourself if you are using a local account.

## Configuring the Mail App

You will see the window below the first time you access the Mail account

Follow these steps to configure it -

**Step 1** – Click on the **Get started** button.

**Step 2** – add the account you wish to use with **Mail** on the next window

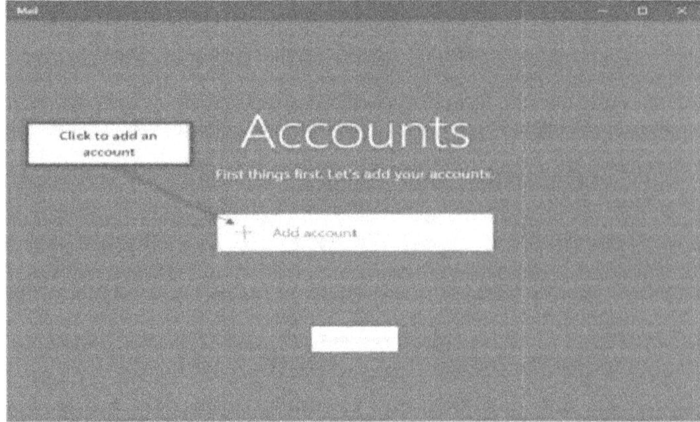

**Step 3** – next when you get to the **Choose an account** window, choose the type of account you wish to configure. The mail app works fine with majority of the mail providers.

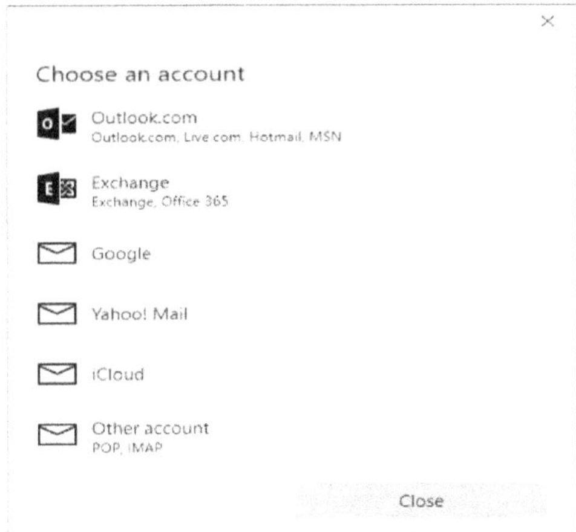


**Step 4** – input your username and password if you're using a Microsoft account.

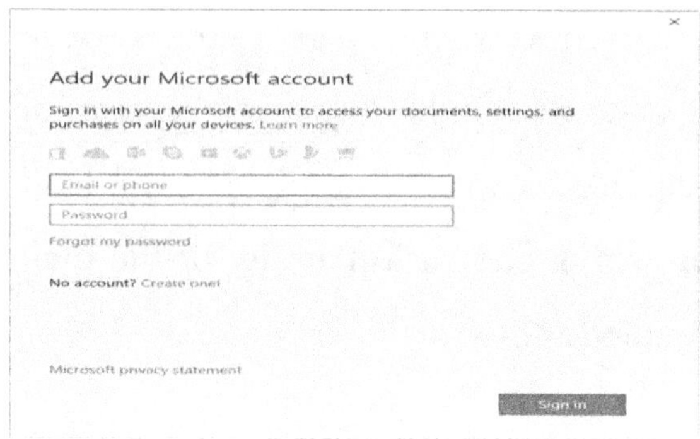

**Step 5** – After a couple of seconds, the **Mail** app will begin to load your emails.

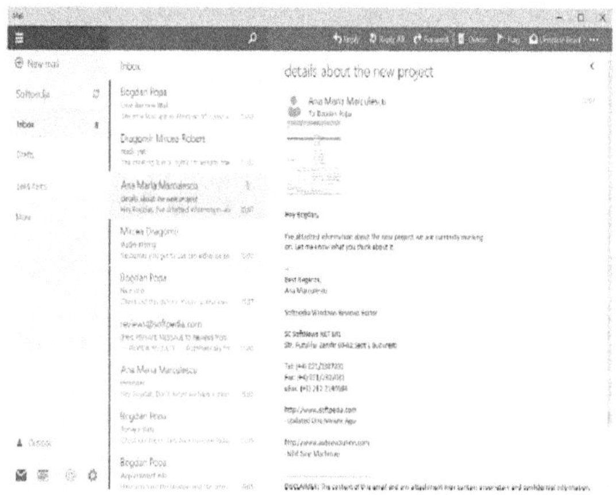

# Chapter 25

# Keyboard Shortcuts

Using keyboard shortcuts is one feature that many Window users finds very helpful. There are many keyboard shortcuts you can use to perform certain tasks faster or make tasks easier.

Majority of the new Windows shortcuts makes use of the Windows key ( ⊞ ) together with other keys to perform lots of tasks. Some of the most useful and common keyboard shortcuts used in Windows 10 re explained below.

| SHORTCUT | ACTION |
| --- | --- |
| Windows key ⊞ | Open the Start menu |
| Windows key ⊞ + S | Open the Windows Search |
| Windows key ⊞ + C | Open Cortana |
| Windows key ⊞ + Tab | Open Task View |
| Windows key ⊞ + D | Show or Hide the Desktop |
| Windows key ⊞ + L | Lock your account |
| Windows key ⊞ + A | Open the Action Center sidebar |
| Windows key ⊞ + I | Open the Settings window |
| Windows key ⊞ + E | Open the File Explorer window |
| Windows key ⊞ + PrintScreen | Takes a screenshot of your whole display and stores it in Pictures > Screenshots |

## Window Snapping

The other type of helpful shortcuts featured in Windows 10 are shortcuts for Window snapping. Windows Snapping was first introduced in Windows 7 and enables you to organize your windows automatically, allowing you to work with several applications simultaneously with relative ease.

Even though you can perform this task with your mouse by moving the windows to both sides of your screen. In Windows 10, you have shortcuts you can use to perform this task.

| SHORTCUT | ACTION |
| --- | --- |
| Windows key + Left arrow | Snap the active window on the left side of the screen |
| Windows key + Right arrow | Snap the active window on the right side of the screen |
| Windows key + Up arrow | Snap the active window on the top of the screen |
| Windows key + Down arrow | Snap the active window on the bottom of the screen |

# Chapter 26

## System Tray

The Notification Area is otherwise known as System Tray, and it is located to the far-right of the Taskbar area. There are different types of alerts and notifications display on the system tray. You can get alert from your computer about your volume level, internet connectivity, and other system notifications

But you can select the type of icons and notifications you want to be display here. The following steps will help you customize your system tray.

**Step 1 –** Open the **SETTINGS** window and select **System**.

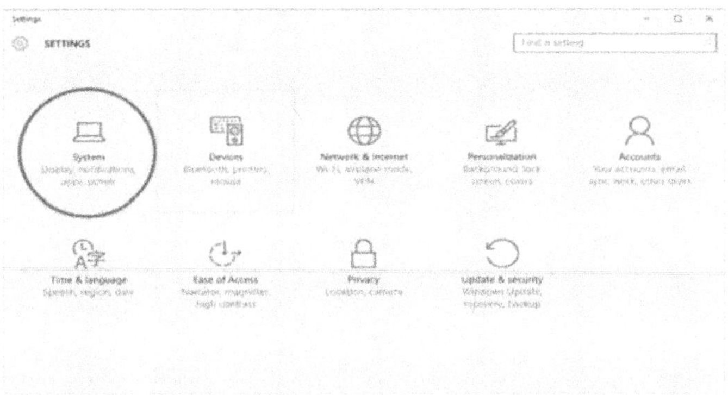

**Step 2 –** Next, choose **Notifications & actions** in the system window. And then proceed to choose the option "Select which icons appear on the taskbar".

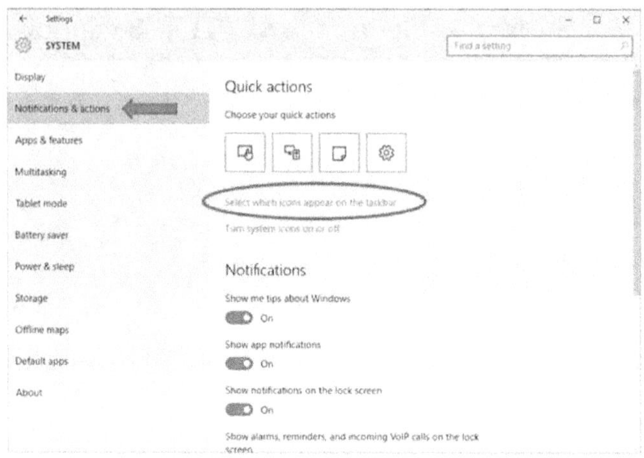

**Step 3** – Next, when you open **SELECT WHICH ICONS APPEAR ON THE TASKBAR** window, here you turn off or on the icons the way you want them.

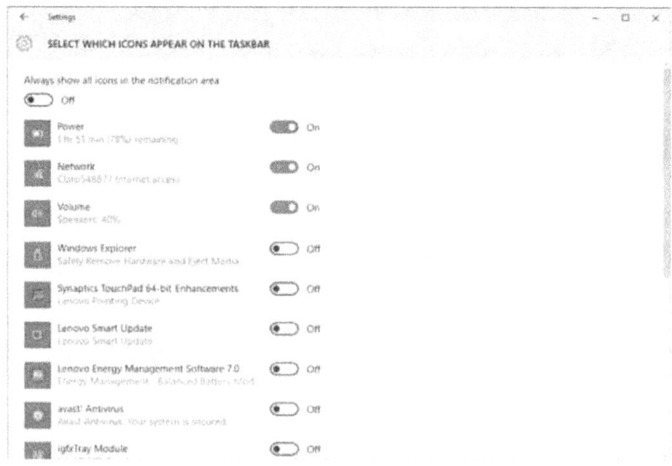

# Chapter 27

# Media Management

Windows 10 allows you to work with your media files (music Videos) in several ways. Some of the functionalities you need to manage your media files have been integrated into Windows to make it easier for you to access them. If you choose a music file for instance, the ribbon below will be displayed on your folder window.

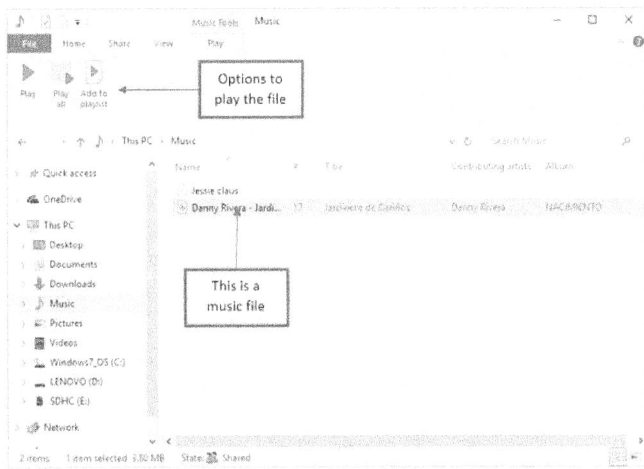

If you select a video file, similar options will be displayed as well.

## Media Applications

Even though your computer has multiple media programs, Windows 10 contains numerous options you can choose from

When it comes to music files, Windows 10 has the regular Windows Media Player, nonetheless, it also contained a new version of Windows media player known as **Groove Music** app formerly known as Xbox Music

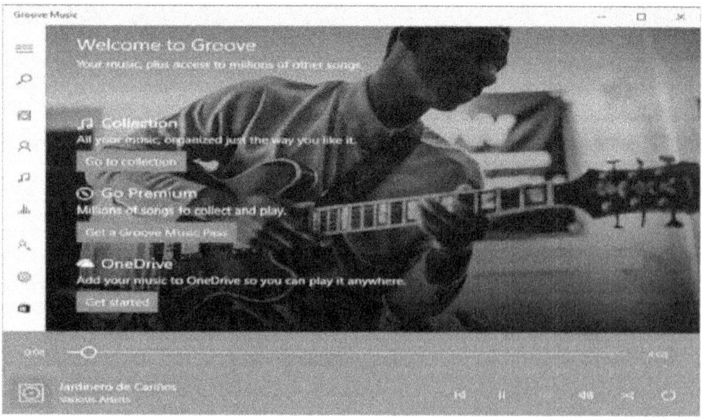

Windows 10 equally uses Windows Media Player for video files, but it now additionally uses the **Movies & TV** app.

There is also the **Windows DVD Player** app in Windows 10 for playing DVD's in your computer system.

Furthermore, you can equally choose the specific application you want to use to open your media files. To do this, follow these these steps –

**Step 1** – Right-click your media file (music or video).

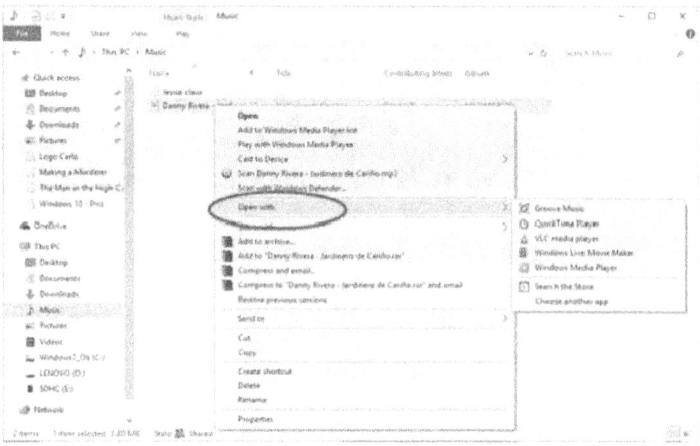

**Step 2** – choose the "**Open with**" option.

**Step 3** – Select the specific application you want to use to open the file.

# Chapter 28

# Favorite Settings

In Windows 10, the new **Settings** app is used for majority of the configurations. While the settings app can be accessed via the start menu without any difficulties, to gain even easier access to your settings app, Windows 10 allows you to pin them to your start menu. When the setting app is pinned to the start menu. It will appear straightaway in the tiles of the start menu

# Pinning your Favorite Settings

The following steps will guide you to "pin" your favorite settings to the Start Menu,

**Step 1** – Go to the Settings window

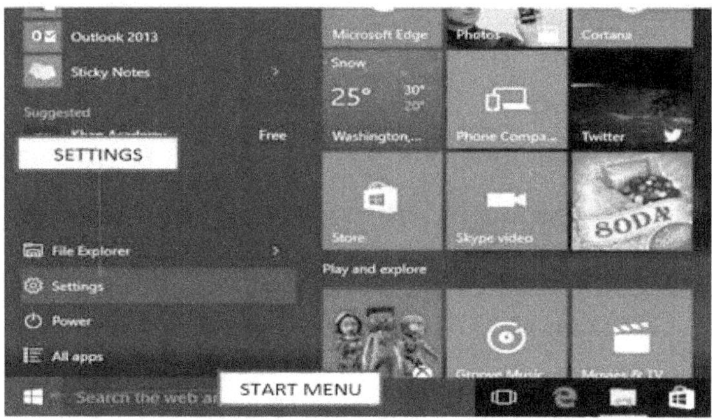


**Step 2** – next when the Settings window is open, select your favorite settings and right-click.

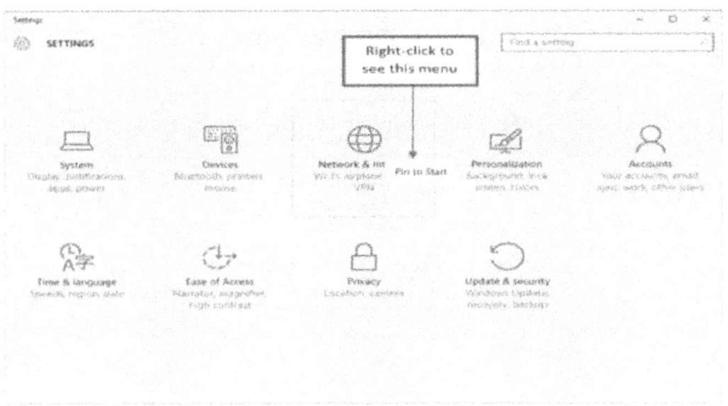


**Step 3** – A small menu will appear choose **Pin to Start**.

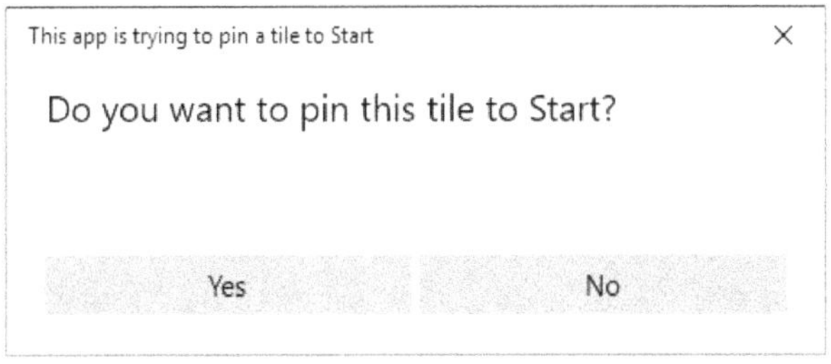


**Step 4** – select **Yes** to confirm your selection. When you have done this, the **Network & Internet** app will be displayed directly on the Start Menu.

You can as well pin more particular setting apps. If you wish to do so, follow these steps –

**Step 1** – Go to the **Settings** window once more.

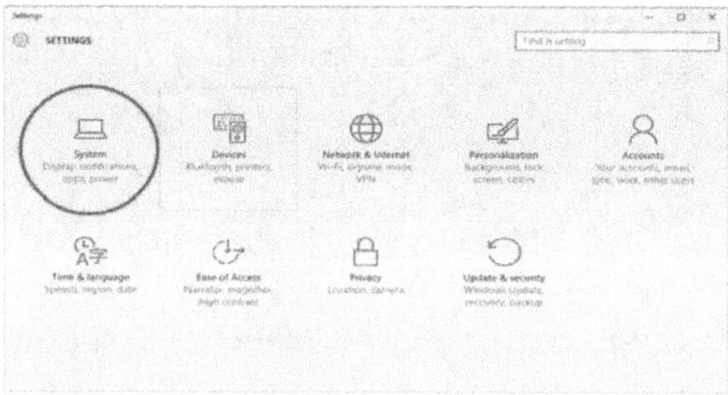

**Step 2** – Click on **System** on the settings window

**Step 3** – Next right-click on **Display**.

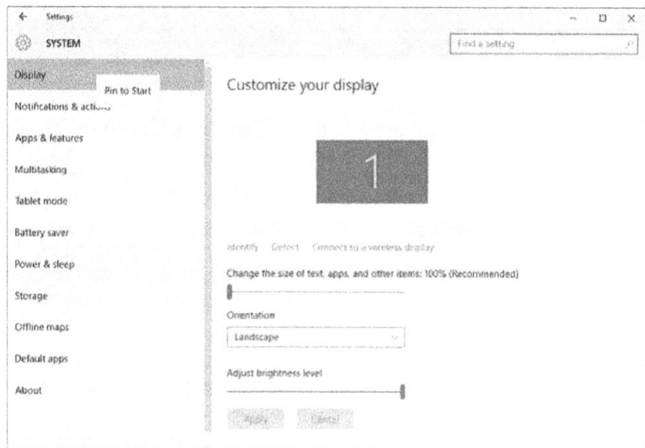

**Step 4** – Next, select **Pin to Start** from the small menu. Like the earlier example, this will pinned the **Display** setting to the Start Menu.

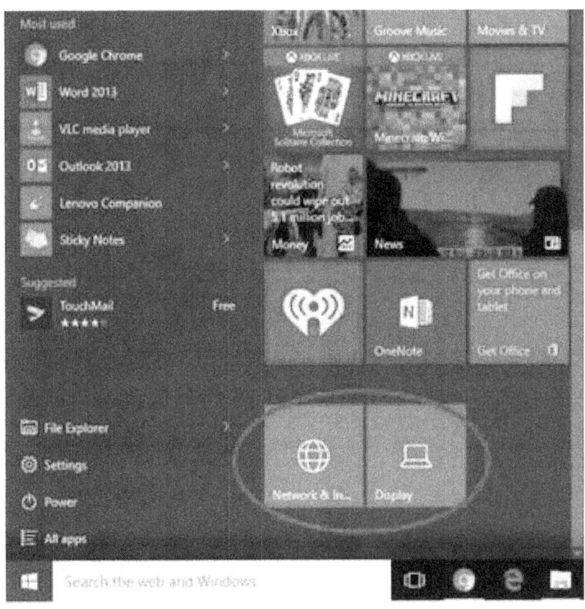

# How to Unpin your Favorite Settings

On the other hand, you can remove or unpinned any pinned app from the Start

Menu simply by right-clicking the app and

selecting **Unpin from Start Menu**.

# Chapter 29

# Shortcuts

A shortcut is a link that points to a program on the the computer. Shortcuts allow you to create links to programs in any folder, Shortcuts allows you to access documents with little difficulty by making those items more accessible, the shortcuts to those items are generally on the desktop, and you can easily identified them by a small arrow at the edge of icon.

**How to Create a Shortcut**

Creating shortcut on the desktop is quite easily, the following steps will guide you-

**Step 1** – Place the pointer of your mouse pointer over an empty space and right-click.

**Step 2** – Select **New** In the menu, and then **Shortcut**

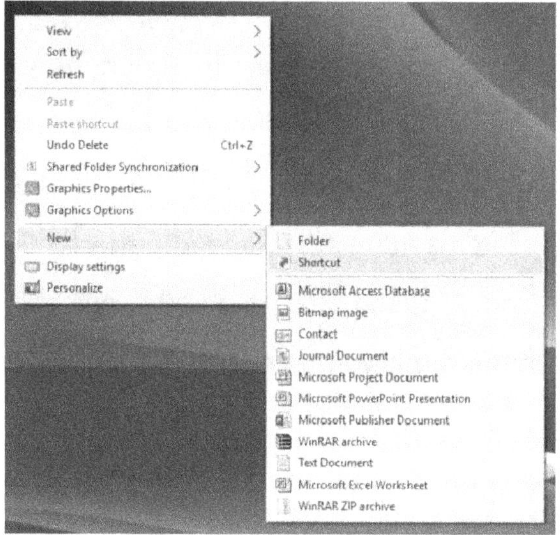


**Step 3** – The next window that will come up is the Create Shortcut window, here you can either type the location of the item you wish to access or Browse it

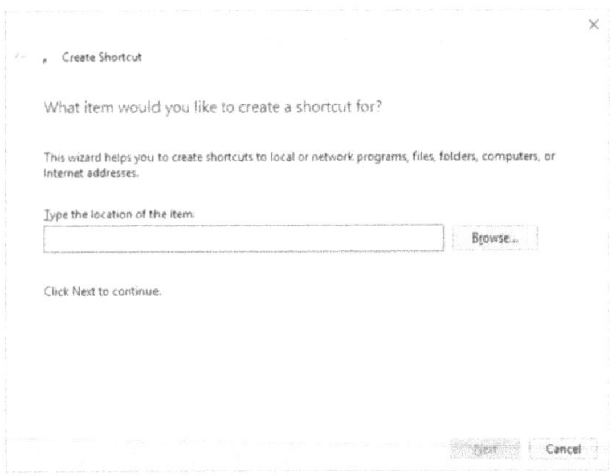

Selecting **Browse** will  bring  up  another window, which will allow you to look for the item in your computer.

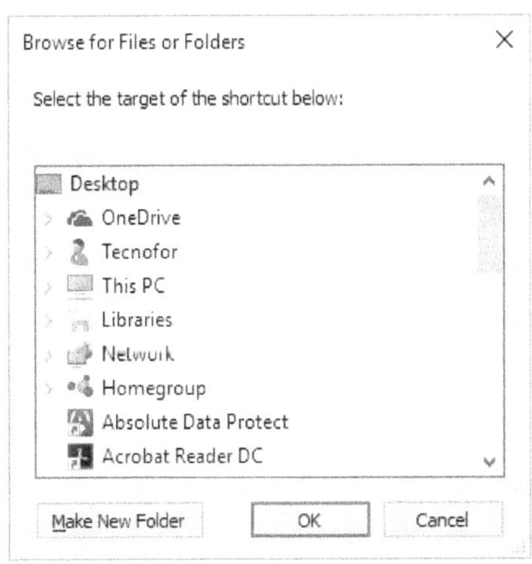

**Step 4** – Once you select the item and click **Next**, you can give the shortcut a name

which you will use to identify in on the desktop

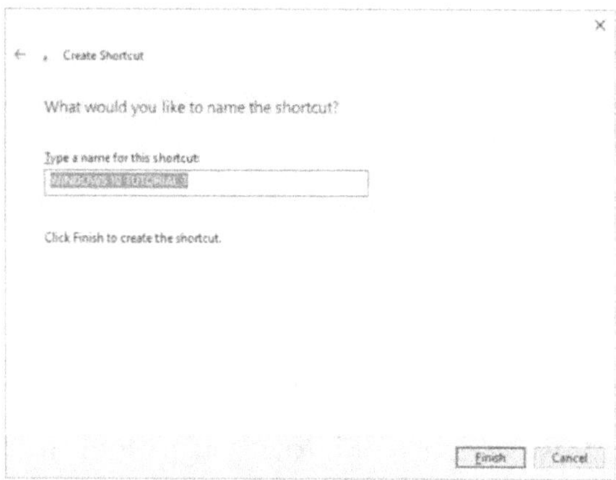

**Step 5** – click **Finish** when you finished making the changes, the shortcut of the file will be display on your Desktop. Note that deleting the shortcut will not delete the original file it access, the file remains in the main folder where it is saved.

# Conclusion

I hope you found this book a valuable resource in your quest to master your Windows 10 OS and enhanced your Productivity. I put this guide together to show you step by step how absolutely everything works with your Windows 10. Hopefully you found this valuable.